THE PHILADELPHIA PHILLIES

A PICTORIAL HISTORY

Veterans Stadium, Philadelphia.

Dedicated to
Robert R. M. Carpenter Jr.
and
Robert R. M. Carpenter III

A.L.

There is no doubt in Tim McCarver's mind what the call should be on this play. And there can be no doubt in the ump's mind how McCarver feels about it.

THE PHILADELPHIA PHILLIES

A PICTORIAL HISTORY · BY ALLEN LEWIS

JCP CORP. OF VIRGINIA

Book and dustjacket design by W. Bradley Miller.

CONTENTS

Bake McBride speeds for the plate, scoring behind Pete Rose while on-deck batter Mike Schmidt gets ready to offer congratulations. In 1980, McBride had his finest all-around season, batting .309, with a career high 33 doubles and 87 runs batted in, second high on the Phillies. He batted over .300 in the World Series, and his three-run homer helped the Phils overcome a 4-0 deficit and beat the Kansas City Royals in Game No. 1. He was the National League Rookie of the Year in 1974 with St. Louis and has a major league career batting average of .300.

Other titles from JCP Corp. of Virginia and Jordan & Company, Publishers, Inc.

The Baltimore Colts: A Pictorial History

The Washington Redskins: A Pictorial History

The Cincinnati Reds: A Pictorial History
   Of Professional Baseball's Oldest Team

The Los Angeles Dodgers:
   The First Twenty Years

The Pittsburgh Pirates:
   A Century Old Baseball Tradition

He Ain't No Bum
   By O.A. ''Bum'' Phillips and Ray Buck

The Winning Tradition:
   A Pictorial History of Carolina Basketball

The Pittsburgh Steelers: A Pictorial History

The Trojan Heritage:
   A Pictorial History of USC Football

The New England Patriots: A Pictorial History

The Real Race:
   The Skip Wilkins' Story (1981 release)

The Cincinnati Reds Scrapbook (1981 release)

Photography Credits

Photos courtesy of the Philadelphia Phillies
Page 2, 3, 4, 5, 14, 20 (top), 29, 30, 32 (top), 34, 37, 38, 39, 42, 47, 62, 72 (top), 73, 77 (bottom), 82, 88, 92 (top), 93, 94, 95, 98, 99, 102, 103, 106, 107, 109, 110, 114 (bottom), 115, 116, 117, 118, 120, 122, 123, 124, 125, 126, 127, 128, 129, 130, 131, 132, 133, 134, 135, 136, 139, 140, 141, 142, 143, 144, 146, 147, 151, 152, 154, 155, 156, 157, 159, 160 (top), 162, 164, 167 (top and middle), 168, 170, 172, 173, 174, 175 (top and bottom left), 176.
From the collection of Bill Loughman
Page 8, 9, 12, 13, 16, 17, 18, 19, 20 (bottom), 21, 22, 23, 25, 26 (top), 27 (top), 28, 32 (bottom), 40, 44, 45, 46, 47 (left), 48, 49 (left), 51, 52, 53, 54, 55, 56, 58, 59, 60, 61, 62, 63, 64, 65, 67, 68, 70, 71, 72 (bottom), 74, 75, 76, 77 (top), 78, 79, 80, 81, 86, 87, 89, 91, 92 (bottom), 96, 97, 100, 101, 104, 105, 108, 111, 112, 113, 114, 119, 121, 160 (bottom), 161, 163.
From the collection of Paul Hill
Page 26 (bottom), 27 (bottom), 35, 36, 49 (right), 64 (top), 83, 84, 85, 165 (top).
Photos by Cheryl Tarlecky
Page 6, 7, 10, 11 137, 138, 148, 149, 150, 153, 158, 175 (bottom right).
Photos courtesy of Citizens Savings Athletic Foundation
Page 24, 33, 43, 49.
Photos courtesy of Camden, New Jersey, *Courier-Post*
Page 165, 166, 169, 171.
Photo by Focus on Sports
Page 166.
Photo courtesy of Richie Ashburn
Page 15.

12

To the victors go the celebration and that's what the Phillies are doing: celebrating in the locker room after their 4-1 victory over the Dodgers to nail down the National League flag. It was on to the New York Yankees and the 1950 World Series.

WORLD CHAMPIONS were the words on the message board. With pure and sudden joy, the agonies, the pains and the frustrations of team and loyal fans were swept away on October 21, 1980. The Philadelphia Phillies — the team that had never quite made it to the top — were suddenly there. They were the champions of the world for the first time in their 98-year history. The sweat of a season's work gives way to tears and champagne in the Phillies locker room. With baseball commissioner Bowie Kuhn (left) and NBC's Bryant Gumbel there, Phillies manager Dallas Green, general manager Paul Owens, and the man who threw the final pitch to win it all — Frank Edwin ''Tug'' McGraw — celebrate baseball's ultimate victory.

INTRODUCTION

There is no one better qualified to write the Philadelphia Phillies story than Allen Lewis.

As a sportswriter for the Philadelphia Inquirer, Allen started covering the Phillies in the pre-Whiz Kid era in 1949 and he continued to follow them for more than 30 years. His knowledge of the game and his dedication to accuracy and fairness have earned him the respect of all of us who have been privileged to work with him through the years.

In this book, *The Philadelphia Phillies: A Pictorial History,* Allen Lewis captures the despair of the Phillies at their worst and the ecstasy of their World Series triumph in 1980.

It is no secret that the Phillies franchise has suffered through some agonizing seasons. The team has had 51 losing seasons this century, including five straight seasons in which they lost over 100 games. In 1961, they set a major league record by losing 23 consecutive games. They blew a pennant in 1964 that was almost impossible to blow and in 1976, 1977 and 1978, they lost all three Championship Series.

The Philadelphia Phillies: A Pictorial History has something for everyone. The book recalls the struggling teams of the formative years before the turn of the century.

Old-timers will enjoy reminiscing in the glory days of Ed Delahanty, Grover Cleveland Alexander, Dave Bancroft, and Chuck Klein, all Hall of Famers.

The not-so-old will be interested in the arrival and development of the Whiz Kids of the Fifties.

And the younger generation can relate to the present-day Phillies.

I joined the Phillies in 1948 as a rookie outfielder out of Tilden, Nebraska, and stayed with them for 12 years. Those 12 years were typical of Phillies baseball; it started with a lot of hope and ended in disappointment.

And while the Phillies haven't always been winners, they've always been interesting and colorful.

In *The Philadelphia Phillies: A Pictorial History,* you'll read about the club owners, the manager, the players and the stadiums — from start to finish.

As a Phillies player for 12 years and a Phillies broadcaster for 18, I wouldn't miss reading Allen Lewis' masterpiece of research in *The Philadelphia Phillies: A Pictorial History.* You won't want to miss it either.

Richie Ashburn

Philadelphia
Base-Ball Club
Photographed by
Gilbert & Bacon

Chapter One

THE EARLY DAYS

While cricket was the more popular sport in Philadelphia for a great many years, baseball markedly increased in popularity in the middle of the 19th century, and in 1866 the Philadelphia Athletics won their first national championship. The Athletics joined baseball's first professional league, the National Association, in 1871 and the Philadelphia Quakers became members in 1873. Both teams played at a field at 25th and Jefferson Streets.

Although the Quakers, regarded as the forerunner of the Phillies, had enjoyed great success, when the National League was formed in the winter of 1876, the Philadelphia franchise was awarded to the Athletics. That team won only 14 of its 59 games and along with the New York Mutuals was expelled from the league for refusing to make the last scheduled Western trip. In the first National League game ever played, Boston beat the Athletics, 6-5, before 3,000 people at 25th and Jefferson Streets on Saturday afternoon, April 22. The only player of note on that first team was outfielder George Hall, who finished as the National League's runner-up in batting average, slugging average and triples and won the first of 21 home run titles collected to date by Philadelphia players. He hit the grand total of five.

Philadelphia was without a National League team from then until 1883 when the franchise in Worcester, Massachusetts, was transferred to Philadelphia. Backing for this club, which inherited no players in the acquisition, was supplied by Colonel John I. Rogers, a Pennsylvania politician and lawyer, and Alfred J. Reach, a former second baseman with the Athletics who made a name for himself through a sporting goods manufacturing firm that bore his name.

The second Philadelphia team in the National League was less successful than the first in its maiden season. Robert Ferguson, who had been player-manager of the team in Troy, New York, the previous season, was named manager but he gave up after the Phillies won only four of their first 17 games and he went into the business office. He was succeeded by Blondie Purcell, an outfielder and pitcher, but the team won only 17 games while losing 81 and finished eighth and last. Pitcher John Coleman won 12 games but set a major league record for the ages by losing 48. The other regular starter, Art Hagan, won just once and lost 14 times, including a 28-0 defeat by Providence that still stands as the most one-sided shutout loss in big league annals.

There was an immediate improvement in 1884 when Harry Wright, who had managed the famed Cincinnati Red Stockings in their glory days and later had piloted teams in Boston and Providence, took over as manager, and pitcher Charley Ferguson was signed. As a 21-year-old rookie, Ferguson, a native of Charlottesville, Virginia, won 21 games in 1884 as the Phillies more than doubled their victory total of the year before and finished sixth. They moved up to third in 1885 as Ferguson and rookie Ed Daily each won 26 games, and the former, who was a fine all-around

Harry Wright piloted the early Phillies teams from 1884-1893. He had managed the Cincinnati Red Stockings and teams in Boston and Providence before coming to Philadelphia. During his tenure, the team moved from the field at 25th and Jefferson Streets to a new home known as Philadelphia Ball Park and later Baker Bowl on 15th and Huntington Streets. Wright is one of two Phillies managers in the Hall of Fame, being selected in 1953.

Charles J. Ferguson came to the Phillies from Charlottesville, Virginia, as a 21-year-old rookie, but he didn't pitch like a rookie. He won 20 or more games for four straight years: 21 in his first season in 1884; 26 in 1885; 30 in 1886; and 22 in 1887. He led the league in earned-run average in 1886 with 1.98. Tragedy struck in spring training in 1888 when he contracted typhoid fever and died.

Dan Casey was one of the Phillies early great pitchers. He was a left-hander and he won 24 games in his first full year, 1886, and came back the next year to win 28.

player, led the team in batting with a .306 average.

Starting in 1885 the Phillies finished in the first division every year until 1896 when they fell to eighth in what was then a 12-team league. Under Wright, who managed until he resigned after the 1893 season, the club came closest to winning the pennant in 1887, finishing only three and one-half games behind Detroit in a gala season that saw the club move into a new park at 15th and Huntington Streets. A showplace at the time, it was opened with a 15-9 victory over the New York Giants on April 30, 1887. It was then known as the Philadelphia Ball Park but came to be known in later years as Baker Bowl after the man who owned the club from 1913 through 1930.

Joining Ferguson, who was a 30-game winner in 1886, were Dan Casey, a left-hander who won 24 games in his first full year in 1886, and Charlie Buffinton, a veteran right-hander who back in 1884 had won 47 games for Boston. In the Phillies' near-miss of 1887, this trio each won more than 20 games pitching primarily to Jack Clements, one of the few left-handed catchers in big league history. Clements played for the Phillies from 1884 through 1897 and caught more than 1,000 games in his 17-year big league career.

With these three outstanding pitchers, it appeared the Phillies might be ready to win a pennant in 1888, but tragedy struck. Ferguson contracted typhoid fever during spring training and died on April 29. To replace him, the Phillies signed William J. (Kid) Gleason, a small right-hander who played through 1912, managed as late as 1923 and was a coach into the 1930s. The loss of Ferguson was too big to overcome, however, and the Phillies dropped to a distant third. The season was marked by the acquisition of Ed Delahanty, one of five brothers who played in the major leagues. Ed played 13 of his 16 seasons with the Phillies and wound up in the Hall of Fame as one of the great sluggers of baseball's early days. The Phillies bought him for $1,900 in July, 1888, and he played second base before later finding a permanent home in the outfield.

Delahanty was the first member of an all-star outfield to arrive. Slugger Sam Thompson came from Detroit in 1889 and promptly led the league in home runs with a healthy total of 20. The next season, Billy Hamilton joined the Phillies from Kansas City and quickly developed into one of the best hitters and base-stealers in history. The threesome played together from 1891 through 1895 and all three hit over .400 in 1894. Still, none led his team because reserve outfielder Tuck Turner, who appeared in 80 games, batted .416 to finish second in the league to Boston's Hugh Duffy, who hit .438, still the major league record.

In 1890 the Phillies finished third, moving up one place, despite losing some players to the newly formed Players League, organized to take advantage of the unrest among the majority of the players. Some of the Phillies who jumped originally were given raises to come back, but lost were their two best pitchers, Charlie Buffinton and Alex Sanders, along with shortstop Billy Hallman, first baseman Sid Farrar, father of famed opera star Geraldine Farrar, and outfielders George Wood, Jim Fogarty and Ed Delahanty. Rival teams also suffered losses and the Phillies managed to win 78 games in 1890, largely due to pitcher Kid Gleason, who won 38 games, and to outfielders Sam Thompson and Billy Hamilton and catcher Jack Clements, each of whom posted batting averages among the top five in the league.

When the Players League gave up after one season, the Phillies reclaimed Delahanty, and he

The Philadelphia Phillies of the National Baseball League — 1886: Top row: Bastian, Clements, Ganzel, Mulvey, Wood and Fogarty.
Middle row: McGuire, Cusick, Irwin, Wright, Andrews, Farrar and Farrell.
Bottom row: Casey, Daily, Ferguson and Titcomb.

Jack Clements, one of the few left-handed catchers in major league history. Clements joined the Phillies in 1884 and caught more than 1,000 games in his 17-year big league career. He was one of the team's two .300-hitters in 1891, batting .310 behind Billy Hamilton's .340.

William J. "Kid" Gleason joined the Phillies in 1888, replacing standout Charley Ferguson who had tragically died during spring training. "The Kid" hit a high-water mark of 38 wins in 1890 and went on to manage and coach as late as the 1930's.

went on to become a great star. Led by their hard-hitting outfield, the Phillies developed into one of the best offensive teams in the league, but their pitching sagged and the club finished fourth every season from 1891 through 1894. After the 1893 season, Harry Wright retired and former Phillies infielder Arthur Irwin was named to succeed him as the manager. He lasted two seasons with the club, finishing fourth and then third in 1895. The 1894 club set several records that still stand. The team batting average was a healthy .343, and on August 17 in a 29-4 victory over Louisville, the Phillies collected 36 hits. The pennant chances of the 1895 club suffered when Gus Weyhing, veteran right-handed pitcher who had won 32 games in 1892, his first year with the club, ran into arm trouble and left the team with only two reliable pitchers, Jack Taylor and Kid Carsey. Offensively, the Phillies dominated the league, leading in runs scored as well as in batting and slugging average. Setting the pace was Delahanty, who batted over .400 for the second year in succession.

The Phillies slumped badly in 1896, finishing eighth in the 12-team league as the pitching staff continued to be a major problem. There were changes in the lineup, too, including two necessitated by an ill-advised trade of outfielder Billy Hamilton because he had sought a pay raise. He was shipped off to Boston in exchange for veteran third baseman Billy Nash, who was named to succeed Irwin as manager. Very little went right for the new pilot: one of his team's 68 losses came in Chicago on a day when Delahanty made baseball history by hitting four home runs in a game. Ed also got a single in that July 13 contest, but the home team won, 9-8.

In mid-August that season, another future Hall of Famer made his debut with the Phillies. Napoleon Lajoie, a throw-in when outfielder Phil Geier was purchased for $1,500 from the Fall River club of the New England League, played first base the rest of that season and into 1897 before being shifted to second base, where he gained his greatest fame. Lajoie batted .361 in his first full major league season, but the Phillies kept sinking and finished 10th under new manager George Stallings, who was to gain renown years later as the manager of the ''Miracle Braves'' of Boston in 1914. But his first term as a major league manager was much less successful and Stallings, who came in with a three-year contract, lasted only half that long. He was a most demanding pilot, even for those times and the players, who suffered under his goading

Ed Delahanty, the $1,900 steal. This man was one of five brothers who played in the major leagues. Ed joined the Phillies in July 1888 — purchased for the sum of $1,900 — and became one of the great sluggers of baseball's early days, being selected for the Hall of Fame in 1945. He batted over .300 for the Phillies for 10 consecutive seasons, 1892-1901, led the league in 1899 with a .410 average, and was the league leader twice in slugging average, .495 in 1892 and .583 in 1893.

Outfielder George "Tuck" Turner compiled the highest batting average in the history of the Phillies in 1894 when, as a reserve outfielder playing in 80 games, he batted .416 to finish second in the league.

in 1897, finally rebelled before one-third of the 1898 season was over. They went to management and demanded a change in what was the first player rebellion against a manager in history. On June 18, the remainder of Stallings' contract was bought up and he was succeeded by Billy Shettsline who, during a long career with the Phillies, filled every job from ticket-taker to club president.

Less than a month after Shettsline took over, Red Donahue, a pitcher obtained by the Phillies after he had lost 33 games for St. Louis the year before, pitched the second no-hit game in the club's history. Charley Ferguson pitched the first back in 1885 in a 1-0 victory over Providence and Donahue beat Boston, 5-0, on July 8, 1898,

Sam Thompson was one of the trio of Phillies all-star outfielders. He came from Detroit in 1889 and showed his power by leading the league that year in home runs with 20. Billy Hamilton and Ed Delahanty were the other two members of the trio. All are in the Hall of Fame, Thompson being selected in 1974.

Centerfielder Billy Hamilton joined the Phillies from Kansas City in 1890. He led the league in batting with a .340 average in 1891 and with .380 in 1893 and was a demon on the base paths, leading the league in stolen bases for four years — 1890-91, 1894-95 — with totals of 102, 111, 98, and 97. He was selected for the Hall of Fame in 1961.

without allowing a hit. Chick Fraser pitched the third at Chicago in 1903 and left-hander John Lush pitched the fourth at Brooklyn in 1906. There wasn't another no-hitter by a Phillies pitcher until Jim Bunning pitched a perfect game against the New York Mets in 1964.

Under Shettsline, the Phillies wound up sixth in 1898, but made a real run for the pennant the next season before finishing third, nine games behind Brooklyn and one in back of Boston. The Phillies won 94 games that year and it wasn't until 1976 that they won more. Wiley Piatt, Red Donahue and Chick Fraser were all 20-game winners in 1899, while young Al Orth, who won 13 of 16 decisions, led the league with an earned run average of 2.49.

Delahanty led the league in hits, doubles, total bases, runs batted in and batting average with his career high mark of .410. Nap Lajoie batted .378, although injuries limited him to playing half a season. Delahanty's new outfield teammates, Elmer Flick and Roy Thomas, each hit well over .300. Thomas, a Phillies regular for nine seasons in a row, was a great leadoff batter who had the knack of fouling off pitches until he found one to his liking, much like Phillies center fielder Richie Ashburn, who came along 50 years later to win two batting titles. Thomas, a native of Norristown, Pennsylvania, came directly from the University of Pennsylvania to the Phillies and played in the National League for 13 years.

The Phillies who landed in third place in 1899. This photograph was taken in early 1898, before George Stallings' contract was bought up and he was replaced by Billy Shettsline. These 1898 players formed the great team of the following year: Back row: McFarland, c; Jamison, p; M. Cross, ss; Cooley, cf; Piatt; p; Douglas, c-1b; Stallings, Dunkle, m; Wheeler, p; Orth, p; Doyle, c; and Lajoie, 2b. Front row: Donahue, p; Lauder, 3b; Flick, rf; Duggleby, p; Abbaticchio, 3b; E. Delahanty, lf; Fifield, p; Elberfeld, inf; and sadly a final unidentified player.

Napoleon Lajoie joined the Phillies in 1896 as a throw-in player when the Phillies purchased outfielder Phil Geier. Lajoie starred with the team for five years, 1986-1900, and was selected to the Hall of Fame in 1937. He led the league in slugging in 1897 with .569, topped the league in doubles with 43 and in RBIs with 127 in 1898.

Chapter Two

NEVER ENOUGH

With the dawn of the 20th century, the Phillies came even closer to finishing on top in 1900, but trouble loomed just ahead with the organization of the American League. The 1900 Phillies got away on top and led the league past mid-June before winding up in third place again, eight games in back of Brooklyn. They posted 75 victories in a season that saw the league reduced to eight teams and the schedule to 140 games. Pitching troubles again plagued the team and Chick Fraser's 16 victories paced the mound staff. Flick led the league in runs batted in with 110, one more than Delahanty who played the entire season at first base before switching back to the outfield.

In 1901, the American League went after National League players in earnest and captured a good many of them by offering sizeable pay increases. Connie Mack, managing the Philadelphia Athletics in the new league, obtained three of the Phillies' pitchers: Chick Fraser, Bill Bernhard and Wiley Piatt. The loss that hurt most, however, was the defection to the A's of second baseman Nap Lajoie.

"It's the Players League fight of 1890 all over again, only worse," said Phillies President John Rogers, who vowed to beat back the new league. The Phillies obtained injunctions against the players who jumped to the Athletics so they moved on to other teams after the 1901 season and for two years were unable to play when their clubs appeared in Philadelphia.

Despite the losses, the Phillies finished second in 1901, seven and one-half games behind Pittsburgh, in a league weakened by the raids. Red Donahue and Al Orth were 20-game winners. Bill Duggleby, whose greatest claim to fame came when he hit a grand-slam home run in his first time at bat in the major leagues in 1898, won 16. Two rookies, Happy Townsend and Doc White, also contributed to make the pitching staff the second best in the league.

Before the next season began, the Phillies lost almost every outstanding player except Roy Thomas to American League teams and they sagged to seventh place. Outfielder Elmer Flick, shortstop Monte Cross, third baseman Harry Wolverton and pitchers Jack Townsend, Al Orth, Red Donahue and Duggleby all left, although a court injunction that year resulted in Fraser, Wolverton and Duggleby returning to the Phillies. Along with the drop in the standings, the club's attendance fell to just over 100,000, a drop of over 50 percent. Reach and Rogers were forced to get a loan from Pittsburgh owner Barney Dreyfuss. Early in 1903, the National League and American League ended their costly war, but Reach and Rogers had been hard hit and, a few weeks after the agreement was signed, they sold the club to James Potter, a Philadelphia stock broker who acted as the head of a syndicate.

Dreyfuss played a part in the sale, making certain his loan was repaid. He also arranged for Chief Zimmer, a reserve catcher on the Pirates, to take over as manager, and for Shettsline to return to the front office after five years in the dugout. The changes did little for the club, however, and the Phillies finished seventh again. Then, too, there was another kind of tragedy. On the afternoon of August 6 a portion of the stands

Charles "Chick" Fraser, with 21 victories in 1899 and 16 victories in 1900, helped the Phillies finish third both years. In 1903, Fraser pitched the third no-hitter in Phillies history.

collapsed, killing 12 and injuring more than 200. Four days later, the Phillies started on a streak of nine consecutive postponements due to the weather — still the longest such stretch in big league history. At this time, the Phillies were slated to play at Columbia Park, located at 29th Street and Columbia Avenue, home of the Athletics, while repairs were being made at their own grounds.

Zimmer was replaced after that one year by Hughie Duffy, who was nearing the end of a career that was to land him in the Hall of Fame. He lasted three seasons. Eighth and last in 1904, the Phillies rose to fourth in 1905 and repeated in 1906, despite losing 11 more games than they won. The 1904 club was the first of 14 in Phillies history to lose at least 100 games, but an important player acquisition that season was outfielder Sherry Magee, who was a standout from his rookie season until he was traded to the Boston Braves after the 1914 campaign. Magee batted .299 in 1905 and formed a potent outfield with center fielder Roy Thomas and right fielder John (Toothpick) Titus, both .300 hitters. Pitcher Togie Pittinger, obtained in a trade with Boston, led the mound staff with 23 victories, followed

Hall-of-Famer Hughie Duffy wound down his career as player-manager for the Phillies in 1904-06.

Sherry Magee joined the Phillies in 1904 and enjoyed a standout career. He is among the team leaders in almost every hitting category and ranks second in stolen bases. His best season was 1910 when he led the league in hitting (.331), runs (110), RBIs (116), and total bases (263).

by Duggleby with 18, as the Phillies returned to the first division.

After the 1904 season, some of the members of syndicate, including Potter himself, decided they no longer wanted to be in the group. They had become discouraged by the many law suits pending as a result of the collapse of the stands in 1903. A reorganization was undertaken and Bill Shettsline took over as president, serving until early in 1909.

The parade of managers continued with the hiring of Billy Murray to replace Duffy after the second consecutive fourth-place finish in 1906. Murray had gained a measure of fame for his ability to handle players while managing the Jersey City club and his 1903 team there set records by winning 24 consecutive games. In his first season, Murray moved the Phillies up a notch to third place, although the only 1907 lineup change was at second base where Otto Knabe, obtained in a trade with Pittsburgh, replaced injured veteran Kid Gleason, who had started his big league career as a pitcher with the Phillies and returned to them in 1903 as an infielder. Pitchers Tully Sparks and Frank Corridon combined to win 40 of the team's 83 victories.

The Phillies fell back to fourth in 1908, but they played a major role in determining the eventual pennant-winner. George McQuillan, a right-handed pitcher who had joined the club the previous September and pitched three shutouts and won four games in just five starts, blossomed into a 23-game winner and Sparks and Corridon won 30 between them. But the pitcher who helped the Chicago Cubs edge out the New York Giants by one game was young Phillies left-hander Harry Coveleski. In the last 10 days of the season, the Phillies and Giants were scheduled to play eight games. Coveleski, a former coal miner from Shamokin, Pennsylvania, had won 22 games for Lancaster before being recalled by the Phillies in September. He beat the Giants three times, earning the nickname of Giant Killer. The New Yorkers won the other five games, but the three they lost to Coveleski by scores of 7-0, 6-3 and 3-2 resulted in their finishing in a tie with the Cubs. Because of that, the disputed Cubs-Giants tie game of September 23, when Giant first baseman Fred Merkle made his famous boner, had to be replayed after the regular season ended. The Cubs beat Christy Mathewson and won the pennant.

Another change in ownership took place before the 1909 season. On February 24, two

Tully Sparks pitched for the Phillies from 1903-1910, winning 15 or more games in 1906-1908 with records of 19, 21, and 16.

The most famous Giant killer in Philadelphia in 1908 was not David but one Harry Coveleski. The young left-hander beat New York three times in the last ten days of the season to rob the Giants of the pennant.

Charles "Red" Dooin went from catcher to manager for the 1910 season, replacing Billy Murray. Dooin was a popular choice and managed until 1914, although he had to be persuaded to keep a bargain-basement pitcher named Grover Cleveland Alexander on the Phillies squad after Alexander's first spring training in 1911.

Philadelphia politicians, Israel W. Durham and James P. McNichol, and a banker, Clarence Wolf, purchased the team and installed Durham as president. Durham became seriously ill before the season opened and went to Atlantic City, New Jersey, but he died there on June 28 without ever seeing his team play. In their last season under Murray, the Phillies slid back to fifth place as George McQuillan fell off to a 13-16 record and the promise Coveleski had given the previous September failed to materialize. The southpaw won only six games and lost 11, went back to the minors and came back to the major leagues in 1914 with Detroit to win more than 20 games three seasons in a row.

After the 1909 season, there was another shift at the top. Horace Fogel, a Philadelphia sports writer, headed a syndicate that bought the team, although Fogel didn't have any money invested. The funds were supplied, it later became known, by Charles P. Taft, brother of the President who already owned the Chicago Cubs. Fogel was a good friend of Charles Murphy, who ran the Cubs for Taft, but his term as president ended in controversy. He was forced to bow out after the 1912 season for making unfounded charges about the pennant race.

Fogel, who realized bucking the popular and successful Athletics for fans was a big order, tried to change the team name from Phillies to Live Wires without success. Early on he decided a change in managers was an immediate priority. He let Murray go, and hired the popular Charles (Red) Dooin, the 30-year-old catcher who had been a member of the team since 1902. Red was a popular choice and he lasted through the 1914 season. His teams finished as high as second once, in the first division three times. He was relieved after bringing the club home in sixth place in 1914.

In 1910 the veteran Earl Moore, who had joined the club in 1908, became a 20-game winner for the only time in his career. Sherry Magee, who had hit only .270 the year before, had the best season of his career, batting .331 to become the Phillies' first batting champion in the 20th century. He also led the league with 123 runs batted in, 110 runs and 263 total bases. Two players who joined the Phillies that season were to play important roles in the club's winning of their first pennant in 1915. In two deals with the Chicago Cubs, the Phillies obtained reserve catcher Pat Moran, who was to manage them to the flag five years later, and then first baseman Fred Luderus, who was a regular through 1919.

Fred Luderus took over chores at first base for the Phillies in 1910. He came from the Chicago Cubs and was to become a hero in the World Series of 1915 when he batted .438 and hit the only Phillies home run in the Series. It came in the fourth inning of the fifth game with no one on base and it gave the Phillies a 3-2 lead over the Boston Red Sox. Boston rallied to win the game, 5-4, and end the Series.

The immortal Grover Cleveland Alexander. He was drafted by the Phillies after he had posted 29 wins for Syracuse in the New York State League in 1910. He came cheaply because other clubs were wary of his enjoyment of alcohol and because he had developed double vision after a blow to the head in 1909. If he came cheaply, he almost didn't come at all. Catcher Pat Moran had to talk manager Red Dooin into keeping the young Alexander on the squad. Alex went on to establish records in every category of pitching, winning 19 or more games in seven consecutive years. His winningest year was 1916 when he posted 33 victories. He was inducted into the Hall of Fame in 1938, the second Phillies player so honored.

Chapter Three

THE ALEXANDER ERA

In the next few years, the Phillies put together a team that finally won a pennant. In February 1911, the Phillies completed an eight-player trade with the Cincinnati Reds that brought another player who was to be a regular on the pennant-winning club. He was George (Dode) Paskert, an accomplished center fielder who was a regular for the Phillies from 1911 through 1917. Infielder Hans Lobert, who later managed the Phillies, also came in the deal and was the regular third baseman until traded to the New York Giants after the 1914 season. He replaced Eddie Grant, the former Harvard graduate who played from 1908 through 1910 and went to Cincinnati in the big trade.

The most important newcomer in 1911, however, was Grover Cleveland Alexander, who was destined to become one of the greatest pitchers in the game's history. The right-hander was drafted by the Phillies from the Syracuse club of the New York State League after he had won 29 games in 1910. He was a bargain buy, reportedly because clubs learned of his fondness for the bottle or because he had suffered from double vision in 1909 following a blow to the head that knocked him unconscious. The double vision lasted less than a year.

In spite of his outstanding record, it took Pat Moran's persuasion to talk Manager Red Dooin into keeping Alex at the end of spring training in 1911. Moran finally convinced Dooin to let Alex pitch against the Philadelphia Athletics in a spring exhibition and the rookie pitched five shutout innings. He went on to win 28 games in 1911 to set a record for a rookie that still stands. He pitched in the National League until 1930, winning 373 games and tying Christy Mathewson for the National League record. Outfielder Cy Williams, who faced both pitchers, said of Alex, "He, too, had that wonderful control. He threw harder than Matty; his curve was sidearmed, almost underhanded, and short and sharp like a slider."

Despite the great first season by Alexander, who led the league in victories with 28 and shutouts with seven, including four in a row in September, and despite a fine performance by Luderus, who batted .301 and finished second in the league in home runs with 16 and third in runs

batted in with 99, the Phillies finished fourth again. Misfortune hit the club hard this season. On May 23 outfielder John Titus suffered a broken leg. On July 10 outfielder Sherry Magee assaulted an umpire and was suspended. On July 26 catcher Charley Dooin suffered a broken leg on a play at the plate. Magee's run-in with umpire Bill Finneran came after he was called out on strikes and was ejected for throwing his bat. Magee hit the umpire on the mouth and was fined and suspended for the balance of the season, although the suspension was lifted in mid-August because of the club's many injuries.

It was more of the same for the Phillies in 1912 when they fell into fifth place, reversing their 79-73 record of the previous year. Pitcher George Chalmers, who had won 13 games in 1911, suffered an injured shoulder, and Alexander, possibly overdoing the bright lights, was slow rounding into form. He won 19 games, his lowest number during his seven-year stint with the Phillies, but he still managed to lead the league in strikeouts and he pitched more than 300 innings, as he did in all seven of his seasons with the Phillies. Magee and Hans Lobert were sidelined for lengthy periods with injuries.

Still, the season saw developments that set the stage for later success. Joining Alex on the pitching staff in 1912 was Eppa Rixey, the 6-foot, 5-inch left-hander from Virginia who was the tallest pitcher ever to be a consistent winner in the first half of the 20th century. Also joining Alex was Erskine Mayer, a right-hander from Atlanta who was drafted off the Portsmouth club and eventually developed into a winning hurler. Then, too, that year saw Clarence (Gavvy) Cravath, a slugging outfielder who had failed in trials with three American League clubs, arrive. He was purchased for $3,500 after hitting 29 homers for Minneapolis in 1911 and he quickly won a job.

It was after the 1912 season that the Phillies lost their president, Horace Fogel, because of his wild charges that the 1912 pennant race had been rigged. He was forced to resign at a November 26 league meeting, and the Cincinnati interests that had backed him wanted to dispose of their investment. A syndicate, headed by William H. Locke, who had been the secretary of the

Clarence ''Gavvy'' Cravath had tried out and failed with three American League teams before he found a home with the Phillies in 1912. It took Cravath little time to make his presence known in Baker Bowl. He led the league for six years in home runs: 19 in 1913; 19 in 1914; 24 in 1915; tied with 12 in 1917; 8 in 1918; and 12 in 1919.

Some of the grand old men of baseball's early years gathered in 1933 to celebrate the 50th anniversary of the Phillies entrance into the National League. Left to right: Chief Bender, Phillies pitcher who is a Hall-of-Famer; Hans Lobert, former Phillies third baseman; Mike Doolan, former Phillies shortstop; Johnny Evers of Tinkers-to-Evers-to-Chance fame; Otto Knabe, Phillies second baseman; Frank Bruggy; Hans Wagner; and Charlie Dooin, former Phillies manager and one-time premier catcher. All except Wagner played for the Phillies.

Pittsburgh Pirates, purchased the Phillies on January 13, 1913. However, Locke died six months later, and the man who had made the second largest investment took over control of the club. He was William F. Baker, a former New York City police commissioner, and he ran the club until he died after the 1930 season.

Under the new ownership, the Phillies showed immediate improvement. In 1913 they led the league for most of the first half of the season and eventually finished second to the New York Giants. It was their best showing since 1901. Alexander won 22 games but was overshadowed by Tom Seaton as the Nebraskan led the league with 27 in only his second big league season. Ad Brennan added 14 victories, but George Chalmers was still bothered by shoulder trouble and won only three. The Phillies blossomed as home run hitters this year, collecting 70 for a total that no club had matched since the turn of the century. The right-handed Cravath had hit 11 the year before, and he led the league this time with 19. The left-handed Luderus, aided by the short right field distance that made Baker Bowl a hitter's

haven, had 18. The right-handed Magee was fourth in the league with 11. The 37 homers produced by Cravath and Luderus were more than any American League club hit and more than all the National League teams except Chicago and Brooklyn. The long-ball power of the Phillies and their climb into contention attracted the fans, and the Phillies drew a total of 470,000, an increase of 220,000 from the year before and a total the club exceeded only once until 1946.

The Phillies had suffered during baseball wars in 1889 when the Players League started and again after the 1900 season when the American League signed stars from the older, established league. It happened again in 1914 with the formation of the Federal League. Second baseman Otto Knabe, shortstop Mickey Doolan, utilityman Runt Walsh and star pitchers Tom Seaton and Ad Brennan were lured away from the Phillies. The contenders of 1913 turned into a sixth-place club in 1914. Although Alexander won 27 and Erskine Mayer blossomed into a big winner with 21 victories, and Gavvy Cravath again hit 19 homers to lead the league and batted

Bill Killefer joined the Phillies at the end of the 1911 season and soon had his hands full. He developed into an exceptional catcher during the era of the hottest Phillies pitchers: Alexander, Rixey, Seaton, and Mayer.

in 100 runs to finish second behind teammate Sherry Magee, they could not compensate for the holes in the middle of the infield. From the best defensive team in the league the year before, they went to the worst and their error total went from 214 to 324. The skid was quickly reflected at the gate as the home attendance fell more than 70 percent to 138,474.

The fall into the second division also cost Red Dooin his job as manager. On October 19 Baker held a dinner for the writers and players in the area and announced that, while he did not put all the blame for the dismal season on Dooin, he felt that Red had lost control of the team and that he was promoting Pat Moran from his coaching job to the manager's chair. ''He knows a lot of baseball, and I think he'll make a fine manager,'' Baker said. That he did is indicated by the fact that in his four seasons at the helm, Moran guided the Phillies to one pennant and two second-place finishes. He moved on to Cincinnati in 1919, again won a pennant in his first season and also finished second twice and third once in his five seasons with the Reds before dying during spring training in 1924.

Soon after Moran was named manager, the Phillies began making other moves that helped them finally win the first pennant in their history in 1915. Three trades helped. One sent popular outfielder Sherry Magee to Boston for George (Possum) Whitted, a speedy outfielder; a second brought third baseman Milt Stock, pitcher Al Demaree and reserve catcher Jack Adams from the New York Giants in exchange for third baseman Hans Lobert; the third saw ex-manager Dooin go to the Cincinnati Reds for Bert Niehoff, a third baseman who was converted into a second baseman by the Phillies.

With a pitching staff that included Alexander, Demaree, Rixey and Chalmers; a top-flight catcher in Bill Killefer, who had joined the Phillies at the end of the 1911 season and gradually developed into an outstanding thrower and receiver; a fine outfield of Cravath, Paskert, Whitted and Beals Becker, obtained in a trade with Cincinnati in 1913, and an infield that included first baseman Luderus, second baseman Niehoff, third basemen Stock and Bobby Byrne, all that was needed was a shortstop. The Phillies found one in the minors.

Dave Bancroft was spotted playing for Portland of the Pacific Coast League by a Phillies scout, who convinced Baker he was worth buying. The native of Sioux City, Iowa, was 23 when the purchase was made and he went on to establish himself as one of the outstanding shortstops of his time during a 16-year career that included four years as a playing-manager of the Boston Braves. A switch-hitter who had fine hands and a strong arm, Bancroft was a cross-handed batter when he joined the Phillies, but he later adopted the orthodox grip. His play landed him a place in the Hall of Fame.

From the start of spring training in St. Petersburg, Florida, Moran sensed that the Phillies were much better than a sixth-place club and he did everything he could to make them winners. Fundamentals were stressed over and over, inside baseball was taught and the players were drilled on a complicated system of signs. Moran worked as hard to steal the signs of the opposition as he did to protect those of his own club. There were even reports that the signs of opposing catchers were stolen by employing binoculars in the center field clubhouse at Baker Bowl.

The National League as a whole was weakened in 1915 by the Federal League player raids and the teams were of nearly equal strength. The

The ill-fated Federal League signed five Phillies prior to the 1914 season including shortstop Mickey Doolan (left). Doolan had been a mainstay in the infield since 1905. His loss, along with second baseman Otto Knabe, left a huge hole in the infield, and the contenders of 1913 sagged to sixth in 1914. The main casualty of this decline was manager Charles "Red" Dooin (top). This ended a career with the Phillies dating back to 1902 that included 1124 games behind the plate, a club record.

The 1915 Philadelphia Phillies — Champions of the National League. Front row — left to right — Becker, Paskert, Moran (manager), Bancroft, Byrne, Cravath. Second row — Dee (trainer), Whitted, Baumgartner, Tincup, Alexander, Killefer, Niehoff, Mayer, Dugey. Third row — Chalmers, Luderus, McQuillan, Burns, Stock, Adams, Rixey, Weiser. Three members of this great team have made it to the Hall of Fame: Grover Alexander, Dave Bancroft, and Eppa Rixey.

Boston Braves and New York Giants were preseason favorites, but the Phillies quickly jumped in front by winning nine of their first 10 games. They held the lead until the Chicago Cubs moved into first place May 22 and led for 40 of the next 51 days. By July 13 the Phillies were back in first place and remained there through the rest of the season. The Braves, who had won the pennant the year before with their amazing spurt in the second half of the season, wound up seven games back in second place, while the Giants finished last but set a modern record by finishing only 21 games behind the pennant-winner.

Anytime the Phillies hit a slump, Alexander would rescue them by coming up with a brilliant performance. The fast-working, sidearming right-hander not only won 31 games to lead the league, but he also led with 36 complete games, 12 shutouts, 376 innings, 241 strikeouts and an earned run average of 1.22 for a National League record that stood until 1968. He started 42 games, and relieved in seven without allowing an earned run. Nine of his 10 losses came in games he started.

Alexander never pitched a no-hit game in his 20-year major league career, but he set a still-standing major league record this season by pitching four one-hitters, three within the span of 31 days. He also hurled three two-hitters, one of which ended in a 1-1, nine-inning tie. His fourth one-hitter was a 5-0 decision over Boston on September 29 that clinched the pennant one week before the season ended and the lone hit was a fourth-inning single by former teammate Sherry Magee. The key hit in the pennant-clinching victory was a three-run homer by Gavvy Cravath in the first inning.

The Alexander-paced pitching staff led the league with a 2.17 earned run average, with 98 complete games and 20 shutouts. Following Alex came Erskine Mayer with 21 victories, Al Demaree with 14, Eppa Rixey with 11 and George Chalmers with eight. The hitting was first-class, too, as the Phillies led the league with 58 homers and missed leading the league in runs by only one. Gavvy Cravath led the league in homers for the third year in a row, this time with a career high of 24 and he also led in runs batted in with 115, in runs scored, bases on balls and total bases. In addition, he became an expert in playing balls off the short right field wall, leading the league with 28 assists. First baseman Fred Luderus came within five points of winning the batting title with a .315 average and was second in doubles with 36 and in slugging percentage to

Cravath. In the World Series, Luderus was the only member of the Phillies to do well. He batted .438 and hit the lone homer for the losers. Cravath, on the other hand, was a big disappointment, getting only two hits for a .125 average, a double in the second game and a triple in the fourth.

The World Series began October 8 on a bright note for the Phillies, but ended in disaster. They won the first game and lost the next four. It wasn't until 65 years later that they won their second Series game. In the opener against the American League champion Boston Red Sox, Alexander beat Ernie Shore, 3-1, on a muddy field. The Phillies scored in the fourth inning when Possum Whitted beat out an infield hit to

The Great Alex. Grover Cleveland Alexander strikes a pose wearing a heavy wool warmup sweater during the 1915 World Series between the Phillies and the Boston Red Sox. Alexander won the opening game, 3-1, and lost the third in Boston, 2-1. The Red Sox won four straight for the World Championship.

bring home Dode Paskert to the delight of the 19,343 fans. The Red Sox tied the score in the eighth. Tris Speaker walked and eventually came home on a single by outfielder Duffy Lewis, who got five hits in eight times at bat against Alexander in the Series. The Phillies came back to score two runs in their half of the eighth — without getting a ball out of the infield. Two walks around an infield hit by Dave Bancroft and an infield out snapped the tie, and the insurance run scored when Luderus beat out an infield hit in front of the plate.

With Alexander scheduled to pitch three of the games, the Phillies felt confident they would win, but Alex lost his second start and was unable to pitch a third time because of back trouble. The Red Sox rolled to the championship, winning four one-run games in succession. The first of those victories came the next day before a crowd of 20,306 that included President Woodrow Wilson and his fiancee, Mrs. Edith Galt. Boston pitcher George Foster singled home the winning

The beginning of the Series. This photo shows fans standing in the grandstand of Baker Bowl as the first game of the 1915 Series, pitting the Phillies Grover Cleveland Alexander against the Boston Red Sox Ernie Shore, gets under way. Alexander took the opener, 3-1.

run in the ninth inning to beat Erskine Mayer and the Phillies, 2-1. Foster allowed just three hits, two of them consecutive doubles by Cravath and Luderus to produce the tying run in the fifth inning after the Red Sox had scored an unearned run in the first. Larry Gardner led off the Boston ninth with a single, advanced on an infield out and scored with two out when Foster singled to center for his third hit of the game.

After an off day on Sunday, the Series resumed on Monday in Boston at the recently constructed park of the Braves, which seated about 8,000 more than the Red Sox grounds. A crowd of 42,300 turned out to see their favorites win again by a 2-1 score, with the winning run coming in the ninth inning for the second straight game. Alexander was beaten by southpaw Dutch Leonard, who pitched a three-hitter. Again it was Duffy Lewis who drove in the winning run off the Phillies star. With runners on second and third and two out, Lewis hit a clean single to center to score the winning run and start a debate

about whether Alex should have intentionally walked Lewis. Alex explained that he thought the next batter, Larry Gardner, was a better clutch hitter than Lewis. In a magazine article during the off-season, Alex wrote, ''I still feel I was right in pitching to him. It may have been the most disastrous decision of my career, but even in defeat my reason compels me to stick by it.''

Lewis was much in evidence again in the fourth game, which also was decided by a 2-1 score. He doubled home what proved to be the winning run in the sixth inning as Ernie Shore defeated George Chalmers. A triple by Cravath and a single by Luderus in the eighth inning spoiled Shore's bid for a shutout before 41,096 fans.

The 2-1 pattern was broken in the fifth and final game after the teams returned to Philadelphia. To the disappointment of the 20,306 fans, Alexander was unable to pitch. Erskine Mayer replaced him, but failed to get through the third inning. The Phillies had a

Baker Bowl and the World Series, 1915. This old photo shows well-dressed and happy Phillies fans flooding the field to celebrate their victory in the Series opener.

Pat Moran made two great contributions to the Phillies. The first was in 1911 when he persuaded manager Red Dooin to take a chance on Grover Cleveland Alexander. The next was in 1915 when as a rookie manager, he led the Phillies to their first pennant.

chance to break the game open in the first inning against George Foster when they filled the bases with none out. But with a 3-2 count on Cravath, manager Pat Moran for some reason ordered a squeeze play. When the right fielder bunted right to the mound, Foster started an easy double play by way of the plate. Luderus then knocked in two runs with a double.

The Red Sox scored once in the second inning and chased Mayer when they tied the score in the third on a home run that Harry Hooper bounced into the temporary center field seats. The Phillies took a 4-2 lead in the fourth on a home run by Luderus over the right field wall and a wild throw by Hooper from right field after singles by Bert Niehoff and Ed Burns later in the inning. Burns did all the catching in the Series because of an injury to Killefer.

Eppa Rixey, who had replaced Mayer in the third inning, blanked the Red Sox until the eighth when Duffy Lewis bounced a game-tying, two-run homer into the center field bleachers. In the ninth, Hooper bounced his second home run of the game into the center field seats for the run that gave Boston the 5-4 victory and the world championship. After the Series, Phillies owner William Baker was criticized for putting extra seats in front of the left and center field bleachers to increase attendance as all three Boston homers went into the makeshift seats on the bounce, a homer under rules at that time.

Each of the Phillies received $2,520.00 as his World Series share and it was a confident bunch that assembled for spring training at St. Petersburg in 1916. It was basically the same team that had won the year before, and the 1916 club actually won one more game but still finished second, two and one-half games behind first-place Brooklyn and just one and one-half games in front of Boston. Alexander had another sensational season, winning 33 games, pitching 38 complete games and 16 shutouts for a record that still stands. Eppa Rixey won 22 games to double his best previous total. Al Demaree added 19 more, but no other pitcher won more than seven, and Erskine Mayer dropped to that figure after winning 21 in each of the two previous seasons. Gavvy Cravath's home run production dropped from 24 to 11, and Fred Luderus hit only .281 after batting .315 the year before.

The Phillies broke even in their season's series with Brooklyn and Boston, but the New York Giants, who finished fourth despite winning streaks of 17 and 26 games, ruined Philadelphia. The Phillies, who led briefly in April, moved into first place in early September before the Giants, who had started their record 26-game winning streak one game before, proceeded to beat the Phillies four straight games. The Phillies stayed close, however, and by beating Brooklyn in a morning game on September 30 took the lead again. In the afternoon game at Ebbets Field, Rube Marquard defeated Alexander, 6-1. Then, while the Dodgers were beating the Giants in a series that brought on charges that the New Yorkers weren't trying, the Phillies were losing three of four doubleheaders to Boston, and that settled the race.

In 1917 the Phillies didn't come nearly as close, although they did finish second again, this time winding up 10 games behind the Giants. With Alexander leading the way as usual, winning 30 games, the Phillies led the league for more than two months. But the Giants moved ahead on June 24. The Phillies stayed close for awhile before fading. They finished with 87 victories, a total they didn't reach again until 1950. The club was not a contender again for a long while. It finished in the second division for the next 14 seasons in succession and for 30 of the ensuing 31 seasons, more than half of that time in the league basement.

Baker Bowl. This was the second home of the Phillies. The park took the place of the original diamond which was on 25th and Jefferson Streets. This field, initially referred to as Philadelphia Ball Park, was opened to fans on April 30, 1887, with a 15-9 win over the New York Giants. It later became known as Baker Bowl for the man who owned the club from 1913 through 1930, William F. Baker, a former New York police commissioner. The Phillies played their last game in Baker Bowl against the same team that they opened with: the New York Giants. The date was June 30, 1938. The picture here is a 1917 post card.

Cy Williams held down center field for the Phillies in 1920 when the entire outfield boasted big names: Irish Meusel was in left and a gentleman named Casey Stengel was in right. Williams led the league in home runs that year with 15, repeated in 1923 with 41 and did it one more time in 1927 with 30, when he was tied for the lead.

Chapter Four

DEEP IN THE SECOND DIVISION

The decline of the Phillies began with the departure of Grover Alexander. With the United States in the war and with the knowledge that the great pitcher was due to go into the Army, owner William F. Baker decided the time was not ripe for taking chances. Fearful that Alex might be injured or killed in the service, Baker traded him and his favorite catcher, Bill Killefer, on November 11, 1917, to the Chicago Cubs for two nonentities, pitcher Mike Prendergast and catcher Bill (Pickles) Dillhoefer and $60,000. Alexander, who won 190 games in his seven seasons with the Phillies, did return from the Army, of course, to win 183 more games before his big league career ended.

While Alexander appeared in only three games for the Cubs in 1918, Prendergast worked in 33, most on the Phillies staff, and his 13 victories matched the total of Brad Hogg. No other Phillies pitcher won more than nine and the worst mound staff in the league contributed to the fall of the club to sixth place with 55 victories. The most notable newcomer, however, was outfielder Cy Williams, the former Notre Damer who was obtained from the Chicago Cubs in exchange for outfielder Dode Paskert. Williams had just turned 30 when the deal was made, but he played 13 seasons for the Phillies, led the National League three times in home runs with a career high of 41 in 1923, and batted .301 in a Phillies uniform. Williams had a swing that was tailor-made for Baker Bowl. He was such a dead, left-handed pull hitter that, in his waning years, opposing teams used to station three infielders to the right of second base and put their three outfielders on a line from center field to the right field foul line in a forerunner of the Ted Williams shift devised by Lou Boudreau a generation later.

The loss of players who went into the service coupled with the departure of Alexander contributed to the lackluster 1918 season. The fact that Moran was unhappy over the Alexander trade and made no bones about it contributed to owner Baker's decision to fire the best manager the Phillies had had in December. For a successor, Baker picked Jack Coombs, a star pitcher with the Philadelphia Athletics in their glory years who was finishing his career with Brooklyn, but his reign was brief. After the Phillies won only 18 of their first 62 games in 1919, Coombs was replaced by outfielder Gavvy Cravath, but the slide to the bottom couldn't be halted, and the Phillies finished eighth for the first time since 1904. Cravath was by now a part-time outfielder and pinch-hitter but this season he batted a hefty .341 and won his fifth and final home run crown with a total of 12 in just 83 games. The only regular to hit .300 was left fielder Emil (Irish) Meusel, who had been drafted before the 1918 season off the Los Angeles club of the Pacific Coast League, and the only pitcher to win more than six games was Lee (Specs) Meadows, obtained in a mid-season trade from St. Louis. He won only eight and was one of 14 Phillies pitchers with a losing record.

The Phillies improved in 1920 but not enough

"Gavvy" Cravath strikes a casual pose for the camera in his last season with the Phillies, 1920. He had begun to write his name in the record books of the National League in 1913 when he led the league in home runs with 19.

to climb out of the cellar. They had a name outfield of Irish Meusel in left, Cy Williams in center and the inimitable Casey Stengel in right. While they led the league with 64 home runs, the pitching still was inept. Lee Meadows won 16 games, George Smith 13 and Eppa Rixey 11 while leading the league in losses with 22. Williams led the league with 15 homers and batted .325 and Meusel hit 14 home runs and batted .309. Early that season, Baker, who admitted he made the Alexander deal because he needed the money, was hard-pressed financially again, and he got $100,000 by trading shortstop Dave Bancroft to the New York Giants for 35-year-old shortstop Art Fletcher and young pitcher Bill Hubbell.

Managers were coming and going in a hurry in these days. Cravath was replaced after the 1920 season by Wild Bill Donovan, a pitcher who had grown up in Philadelphia, pitched in the major leagues for almost two decades and had managed the New York Americans from 1915 through 1917 without much success. Donovan stayed around for 102 games and was replaced by Irving (Kaiser) Wilhelm, another former pitcher. The Phillies improved slightly under Wilhelm and moved up to seventh in 1922 after another eighth-place finish in 1921. Neither ex-pitcher was able to solve the club's mound woes, although Lee Meadows and Jimmy Ring, who had come from Cincinnati in a trade for Eppa Rixey after the 1920 season, were respectable workmen. For the fourth year in a row the Phillies led the league in home runs in 1922 and their increasing yearly totals were a reflection of the changes coming to pass because of the introduction of the lively ball. They had 42 in 1919, then 64, 88 and 116 and led again in 1923 with 112. None of the 116 homers in 1922 was hit in an August 25 game that made history. That afternoon in Chicago, the Cubs beat the Phillies, 26-23, in the highest-scoring big league game ever played. The Cubs scored 10 runs in the third inning and 14 more in the fourth for a 25-6 lead.

Art Fletcher, who closed out his playing career by playing in 110 games in 1922, was named to succeed Wilhelm as manager after the 1922 season. He lasted four seasons, but the best the

fiery ex-shortstop could do was a tie for sixth while finishing seventh once and eighth twice. Pitching was the usual weakness during his tenure, although Jimmy Ring did manage to post a remarkable 18-16 record for a team that won only 50 games in 1923, and Hal Carlson, a 28-year-old former Pittsburgh Pirate, had a fine 17-12 log for the 1926 cellar-dwellers.

Another former member of Connie Mack's great Athletics teams was the manager in 1927. Stuffy McInnis, the first baseman on the famed $100,000 infield, suffered through 103 defeats and a cellar finish in his only major league managerial venture. Cy Williams was a standout again this year. He tied Hack Wilson of the Chicago Cubs for the home run title with 30 but the Phillies' pitching kept getting worse.

One of Williams' fondest memories was of a 1927 game with Remy Kremer pitching for the pennant-bound Pittsburgh Pirates. With the Phillies trailing, 1-0, in the last of the ninth inning, Cy walked up with a man on base and

Brooklyn Dodgers manager Wilbert Robinson (left) is dressed more like a banker than a baseball team manager as he poses with Phillies manager Art Fletcher just before the 1925 season opener at Ebbets Field in Brooklyn. The Dodgers took the game, 3-1.

was certain Kremer would throw him a fast ball
on a 3-2 pitch, and he did three times in a row.
All three times Williams hit the ball over the
right field wall, but the first two curved foul. The
third won the game. ''And I never did touch the
plate,'' Williams recalled some years later. ''By
the time I reached second base, the crowd rushed
out and carried me off. That was my
unforgettable homer.''

Home attendance reached 305,120 in 1927,
despite a near calamity. On Saturday afternoon,
May 14, during a game with St. Louis, a section
of the stands collapsed. There were no serious
injuries but the Phillies had to play their next 12
games at Shibe Park, home of the Athletics.

Since the firing of Pat Moran after the 1918
season, the Phillies had employed six different
managers in just nine seasons, but that trend
slowed with the hiring of Burt Shotton in
November, 1927. He was a former major league
outfielder who had served as an aide to Branch
Rickey in St. Louis and had spent the two

It looked more like sandlot baseball than the major league
brand, but it was the Phillies taking batting practice at a
field in Bradenton, Florida, during spring training in March
1927.

previous seasons managing the Syracuse farm club of the Cardinals. Shotton stayed with the Phillies for six years, longer than any other manager until the 1960s. Under his guidance, the Phillies made their best showings since Pat Moran's days, finishing fourth, fifth, sixth, seventh and eighth twice. More than a decade later, Shotton managed the Brooklyn Dodgers to two pennants.

In 1928 — Shotton's first season, the Phillies finished last for the third straight year and made their poorest showing in 45 years, but that season marked the arrival of a player who was to become a star and eventually was elected to the Hall of Fame. His name was Chuck Klein, and he became a member of one of baseball's greatest slugging threesomes. The first member of that trio to arrive was first baseman Don Hurst, who came with Shotton from Syracuse after the 1927 season. Klein, who had been a star high school athlete in Indianapolis, was purchased in July, 1928, from the Fort Wayne club of the Central League for $7,000. He had played only 102

A manager's welcome of two Florida beauties and a floral horseshoe was what greeted Phillies manager "Stuffy" McInnis when the team opened their 1927 spring training in Bradenton, Florida. A group of townspeople had marched to the practice field on the opening day of training and the town presented the flowers.

minor league games at the time but had shown the slugging ability that was to make him a star. The final member of the threesome was Frank (Lefty) O'Doul, a former pitcher who had switched to the outfield and played for the New York Giants in 1928 until traded to the Phillies along with $25,000 for outfielder Fred Leach that October. That trio came together in 1929, but in 1928 the Phillies were just another bad team, especially on the mound where rookie Ray Benge was the team's leading pitcher with an 8-18 record and an earned run average of 4.55.

There were some other outstanding hitters on that 1929 team that climbed up to fifth place, the best showing by the Phillies since 1917, but Hurst, right fielder Klein and left fielder O'Doul were the most feared. The three combined to hit 106 home runs. No other team in the history of baseball, except the 1927 New York Yankees, had ever had three players combine for 100 up to that time. All three were left-handed batters who took full advantage of the short right field wall. In his first full season, Klein set a National

League record with 43 homers, and might have topped the 50 mark had not Baker decided to add 15 feet to the top of the right field wall because, he said, ''home runs had become too cheap.'' O'Doul, who never again came close to such a total, hit 32, and Hurst had 31. The team set a National League record with 153. Homers weren't all that team hit. O'Doul won the batting title with a .398 average, missing the .400 mark by just one hit and collecting 254 hits for a National League record that has never been surpassed. Klein batted .356, catcher Virgil (Spud) Davis .342, third baseman Pinky Whitney .327, second baseman Fresco Thompson .324, center fielder Denny Sothern .306, Hurst .304, and utilityman Barney Friberg, .301 in 128 games. With four players batting in more than 100 runs each — Whitney joining the trio — the Phillies tied a National League record that still stands. As a team, they led the league with a .304 batting average and a .467 slugging percentage. All that offense couldn't make up for the pitching problems, although the

Lefty O'Doul was one of the Phillies memorable slugging threesome in 1929-30. He joined with Chuck Klein and Don Hurst to literally run away with many of the league's hitting marks. He was a pitcher turned outfielder, but mostly turned batter. He led the league in 1929 with a .398 average and 254 hits.

Chuck Klein and Jimmy Foxx were the kings of clout in Philadelphia in the late 1920's and 1930's, Klein with the Phillies and ''double xx'' with the A's. In 1929, Klein set the National League home run record with 43. Later, in 1932, each won the Most Valuable Player award for his league. Foxx wound up his career as a Phillie in 1945.

Phillies did have three hurlers who won more than 10 games, led by Claude Willoughby, who posted a 15-14 record, the best of his career.

As potent as their attack had been in 1929, it was even more devastating in 1930, and yet the Phillies fell back to the cellar because the pitching was the worst ever seen on a big league team. The team earned run average of 6.13 in 1929 went up to 6.71 in 1930, although Fidgety Phil Collins, in his second year with the club, managed to win 16 games while losing only 11. Ray Benge posted an 11-15 record for the second straight season, but Claude Willoughby had a 4-17 log and Les Sweetland 7-15. Half of the six regular pitchers had earned run averages over 7.50. The offense produced 47 more runs than the year before and the team batting average soared to .315, but was only the second highest in the league as batters enjoyed the most productive season in history. Klein led the way with a .386 average, 40 homers and 170 runs batted in, while O'Doul checked in with .383, 22 and 97, and Hurst .327, 17 and 78. Pinky Whitney batted .342 and knocked in 117 runs, Spud Davis hit .313 and Barney Friberg .341. The Phillies averaged better than six runs per game but their pitchers gave up better than seven and one-half runs. Particularly in Baker Bowl, high-scoring games became routine, and that was the only park in which there was not a single shutout pitched. The average score of the 77 games played at Baker Bowl that year was 8-7 in favor of the opposition.

Don Hurst was the third member of one of the most potent outfields in baseball history. In 1929, he, Klein, and O'Doul became the second trio from one team to hit more than 100 homers in a season.

William F. Baker, president of the Phillies from 1913 through 1930. Baker died suddenly on December 4, 1930, of a heart attack in his room at the Ritz-Carlton in Montreal, Canada. He was in Canada with his wife to attend the annual meeting of the National Association of Minor Leagues.

Pinky Whitney was one of the mighty bats during the Phillies grand days as an offensive powerhouse. Whitney played third base from 1923-1933 and again from 1936-1939. He was consistently near or over .300 as a batter and he hit .342 in 1930.

Chuck Klein could do it all and here he displays one of the rewards of baseball greatness: the Most Valuable Player Award in 1932. He received that award from both the Baseball Writers Association and from the Sporting News. He was also the Sporting News' MVP in 1931. He came to the Phillies as an outfielder in 1928 and became one of baseball's great sluggers. Klein led the league in 1933 with a .368 average. he led the league twice in hits: 226 in 1932 and 223 in 1933. A power hitter, he led the league in homers for four years, 1929 and 1931-1933, setting his personal mark of 43 in 1929.

Chapter Five

THE EDGE OF BANKRUPTCY

While attending the minor league meetings in Montreal after the 1930 season, William F. Baker had a heart attack and died the morning of December 4. Lewis Charles Ruch, who had joined with Baker in buying shares in the club back in 1913 and had served as vice president, was elected as the new club president on January 7, 1931, and he served for the next two seasons. Baker's will left a large block of stock to his long-time secretary, Mrs. May Mallon Nugent, who had become club secretary. When Mrs. Baker passed away soon after her husband, she also left her stock to Mrs. Nugent and her son, Gerald, Jr. Mrs. Nugent's husband, Gerald Nugent, a former shoe salesman who joined the organization and had been named business manager in 1927, replacing William Shettsline, succeeded Ruch as president in November, 1932. He held the job for just over a decade during which time the Phillies were constantly struggling to meet their financial obligations. This was even more pronounced than during Baker's regime. One way this was accomplished was by trading away the best players for lesser ones, with a sizeable amount of money accompanying every deal.

Before Baker died, he traded Lefty O'Doul and Fresco Thompson to Brooklyn for pitcher Jumbo Jim Elliott and others and dealt shortstop Tommy Thevenow and pitcher Claude Willoughby to Pittsburgh for shortstop Dick Bartell in one of the club's best trades. When Nugent was in control, he sent pitcher Ray Benge to Brooklyn after the 1932 season and on June 17, 1933, traded third baseman Pinky Whitney to the Boston Braves.

The blockbuster was still to come. On November 21, 1933, Nugent traded Chuck Klein to the Chicago Cubs for three nonentities and the inevitable check, this one for $65,000. Klein played on a bad leg for the Cubs and was a disappointment, eventually coming back to the Phillies. His departure to Chicago was followed the next June by that of Don Hurst, who proved more of a disappointment than Klein. Nugent was either lucky or smart in the lesser players he obtained in his trades. In the Hurst trade, he got first baseman Dolf Camilli, a youngster who developed into a standout and was used in a later trade in less than four years, in addition to

$30,000.

In 1931 the Phillies moved up to sixth place, helped by the 19 games Jumbo Jim Elliott won in his maiden season with the club. In 1932 Shotton was regarded as something of a miracle man when the Phillies finished fourth after 14 consecutive second-division finishes. In this season, the Phillies had six pitchers who won 10 or more games, while the potent offense led the league in runs scored, home runs and batting and slugging averages. Don Hurst led the league with 143 runs batted in, while Klein finished second with 137 and Pinky Whitney third with 124. Klein hit 38 homers to tie New York Giants star Mel Ott for the league title, and six regulars, including Klein and Hurst, as well as rookie outfielder George (Kiddo) Davis, outfielder Hal Lee and shortstop Dick Bartell hit over .300.

The Phillies fell back to seventh place in 1933

Dick Bartell (left), captain of the Phillies in 1933, gets an assist from Glenn Wright, captain of the Brooklyn Dodgers, as they raise the flag at Baker Bowl before the opening game of 1933.

and attendance, which had been over 268,000 for four straight seasons, dropped to less than 157,000. Nugent decided changes had to be made and more funds were needed. He fired Shotton and traded Klein. Nugent picked Jimmie Wilson to replace Shotton. Wilson, a Philadelphia-born catcher who had joined the Phillies in 1923, was traded in 1928 to St. Louis, where he developed into a star, and then returned to the Phillies on November 15, 1933, as player-manager. That trade had sent catcher Spud Davis to the Cardinals and brought $30,000 to the Phils.

The deal that sent Klein away was difficult for long-time Phillies fans to accept. The red-faced slugger was a 6-foot, 185-pounder who could do everything asked of an outfielder, including run and throw. He led the league in stolen bases in 1932 and twice led the league in assists by an outfielder, including in 1930 when he had 44 for a major league record that still stands, having mastered the art of playing the caroms off the right field wall. In 1932 Klein was named the National League's Most Valuable Player, the first of only three Phils to be so honored in the last half a century. From 1929 through 1933, Klein had 200 or more hits every year, led the league in runs scored three times, in doubles twice, in home runs four times, in runs batted in twice and won the Triple Crown in 1933 when he batted .368. Klein's first five full seasons in the major leagues may well be the best of any player who ever lived.

In 1934, the club's first season with Jimmie Wilson as the manager, the Phillies finished seventh, escaping another cellar finish only because of the fine pitching of Curt Davis, a right-hander obtained the previous fall in the draft. Davis won 19 games and his 2.95 earned run average was not only third best in the league but the lowest for any regular Phillies pitcher since 1920. One other development marked that season: Sunday baseball was finally legalized in Pennsylvania for the first time. Still, the Phillies drew only 13,500 more than the year before, and the 169,885 home total would be a bad week for the club nowadays.

Season Opener. Philadelphia mayor J.H. Moore prepares to throw out the first ball on opening day of the Phillies 1933 season. From left: Brooklyn Dodgers manager Max Carey, Mayor Moore, Phillies president Gerry Nugent, and Phillies manager Burt Shotton. The Dodgers took the opener, 5-4.

It was one of Pennsylvania's first Major League Sunday games and the opponents were Philadelphia's two teams. Jimmie Wilson (left) of the Phillies and one of baseball's giants, Connie Mack, wish each other luck before the game. Mack's wish to Wilson carried the day as the Phillies won, 8-1, in this April, 1934, contest.

Fast trades and deals for cash, as well as players, was one of the ways that the financially weak Phillies stayed afloat in the 1930s. Here Arthur "Pinky" Whitney, captain and third baseman for the Phillies (third from left) and Phillies left fielder Hal Lee (second from left) signify their being traded in June, 1933, to the Boston Braves by exchanging uniforms with Wes Schulmerich (left) and Fritz Knothe (right). In addition to sending Schulmerich and Knothe to the Phillies, the Braves also paid the Philadelphia club an undisclosed amount to cash.

Dolf Camilli, a star Phillies first baseman, is shown during 1936 spring training at Winter Haven, Florida. Not just a good defensive player, Camilli poses with a bat that he knew how to use during his years with the Phillies. He hit .315 in 1936 and .339 in 1937. Standing with Camilli are (left to right) Chicago Cubs Charlie Grimm and Phil Cavarretta.

The Phillies leading pitchers put their heads and their baseballs together at the start of spring training in Winter Haven, Florida, in March 1935. Shown (left to right) are Syl Johnson, Curt Davis, Euel Moore and Phil Collins.

In the fall of 1934, Nugent swapped shortstop Dick Bartell, who had developed into a star and had batted a combined .295 in his four years with the Phillies, for four players and the $50,000 he needed to continue operating the club. With Davis winning 16 games and Camilli hitting 25 homers, the Phillies finished seventh again in 1935. After that campaign the club traded catcher Al Todd to Pittsburgh for $20,000, catcher Earl Grace and rookie pitcher Claude Passeau, who developed into a standout and, of course, was traded after just over three seasons. In May, 1936, Nugent reclaimed Klein in a trade that sent pitcher Curt Davis to Chicago for the outfielder, pitcher Fabian Kowalik and $50,000, but the Phillies dropped into the cellar despite the fact that Camilli and Klein both hit over .300 with at least 20 homers. Claude Passeau won 11 games as did Bucky Walters, a Philadelphian who had been converted with excellent results from a third baseman into a pitcher by Manager Jimmie Wilson. Klein put his name into the record books that season on July 10 when he hit four home runs in Pittsburgh's Forbes Field, only the fourth player to accomplish the feat at the time and the second in the 20th century. The fourth homer was hit in the 10th inning to help the Phillies win.

When the Phillies finished seventh again in 1937, Nugent went back to trading players to survive. He dealt Dolf Camilli to Brooklyn in March and swapped Bucky Walters to Cincinnati in June, receiving one player in each deal as well as $50,000 and $55,000. Both Camilli and Walters helped their new clubs win pennants

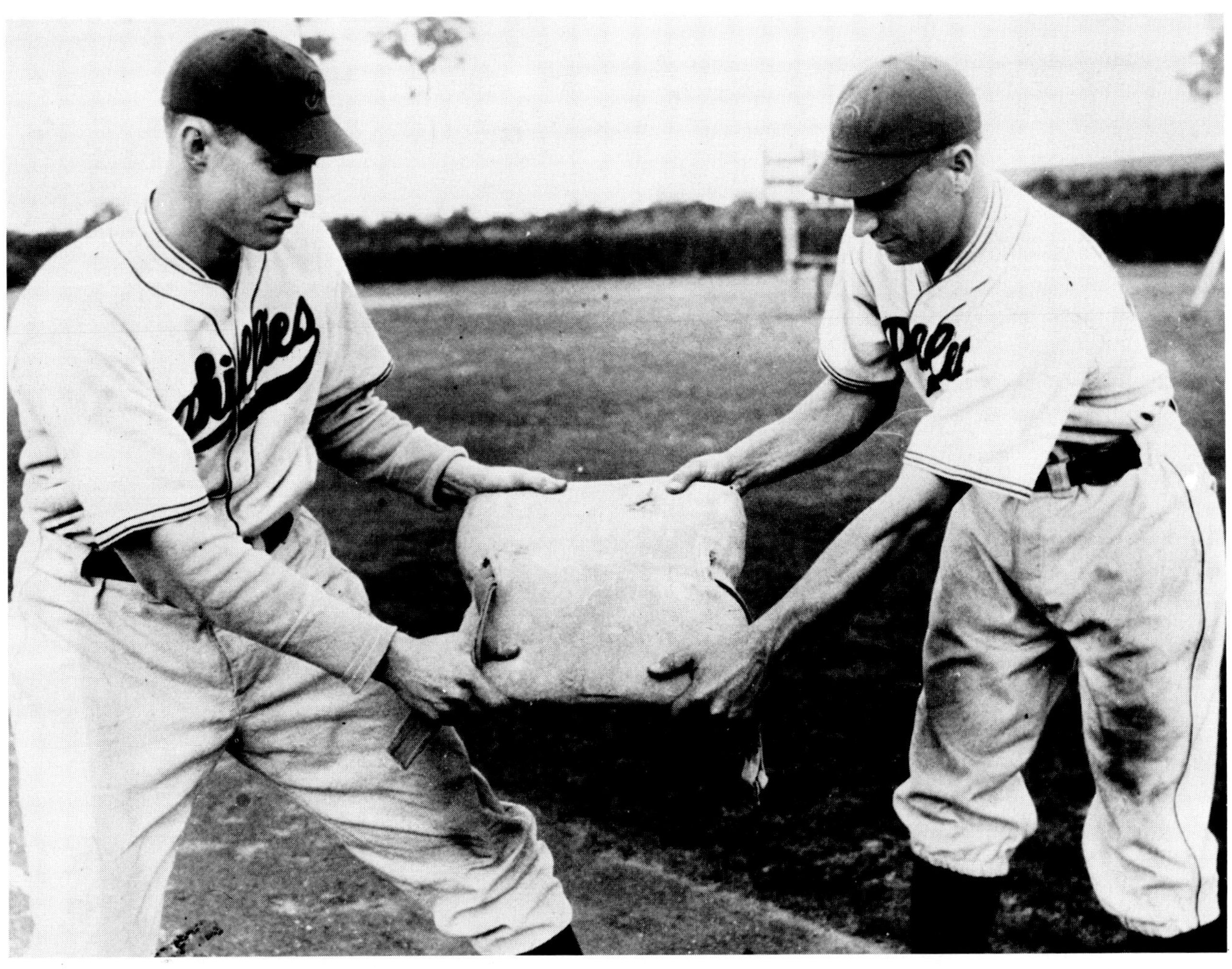

Bucky Walters (left) and Johnny Vergez strike a fighting pose over the third base position for the Phillies in spring training in 1935. Walters had held the position in 1934, batting .250. Vergez got the nod for 1935, and he batted .249. Walters was converted with great success into a pitcher for the Phillies.

Gerry Nugent (left), president of the Phillies, talks with
Phil Wrigley, owner of the Chicago Cubs, during a meeting
of the National Baseball League in New York in December
1936. Nugent had been a shoe salesman before joining the
Phillies organization in 1927. He became club president in
1932. His wife and son had been left substantial stock in
the Phillies by William Baker, one of the earlier owners.
Mrs. Nugent had been Baker's long-time secretary before
his death. Nugent served as president for more than 10
years, during which time the Phillies were always
struggling financially.

A run scores for the Phillies in 1936. Morry Arnovich
slides safely home to score for the Phillies as catcher
Jimmie Wilson steps away from the plate before taking his
turn in the box. Phillies outfielder Lou Chiozza is giving the
"safe" sign for his teammate.

before the start of World War II. By this time, Wilson was becoming discouraged. When the Phillies finished eighth in 1938, he quit with two games remaining in the season. The 1938 season was notable because the Phillies finally abandoned Baker Bowl, moving seven blocks west to Shibe Park, the home of the Athletics, where they remained until moving to Veterans Stadium in 1971. The Phillies, who played in Shibe Park previously when Baker Bowl was being repaired, played for the first time as permanent tenants there on July 4, 1938, beating the Boston Braves in the second game of a doubleheader after losing the first game.

With the departure of Wilson, James T. Prothro, known as Doc because he was a dentist in Tennessee, was named manager. He had won Southern Association pennants at Memphis and Little Rock and was regarded as a good baseball man, but he had nothing to work with on the Phillies. The three Phillies teams he managed finished last and each lost more than 100 games. The advent of night home games in May, 1939, resulted in a temporary increase in attendance but not in the number of victories and Nugent was still busy trading away his players. In late May, 1939, he swapped pitcher Claude Passeau to the Chicago Cubs for $50,000 and three players, including young pitcher Kirby Higbe, who developed into a standout and was traded to Brooklyn for $100,000 and three players after the 1940 season. In 1941, the Phillies lost the most games in their history, a whopping 111, and did not have a pitcher who won more than nine games. After losing 320 games in his three seasons at the helm, Prothro was succeeded by Hans Lobert, who had played and coached for the Phillies. His 1942 team promptly lost 109 games and the club finished last for the fifth year in a row.

Despite all his wheeling and dealing and his ability to obtain good young players as well as cash in his many trades, Nugent wasn't able to keep the Phillies from falling deeper and deeper into debt. Finally, in February, 1943, the National League took over the franchise and began looking for a buyer. They found one that same month in a syndicate headed by William D. Cox, a New Yorker who was president of a firm of lumber brokers. His term as president of the Phillies lasted only one season.

Very quickly, Cox hired veteran manager Bucky Harris to run the Phillies and he also managed to assemble a wartime team that was a slight improvement over the teams of the recent

In the 1930s, Wheaties joined gum and tobacco in the race for the baseball fan's heart and purse by offering collectibles. This example from a Wheaties box is of the Phils Johnny Moore.

past. Cox, who worked out with the club at times during spring training that year at Hershey, Pennsylvania, considered himself something of a baseball expert because he had played the game briefly while attending Yale University. He often traveled with the team and was free with his advice to Harris, who had difficulty concealing his dislike for the owner. One day after a loss, Cox stormed into the clubhouse and began talking in loud tones about his misfit players, referring to them as ''those jerks.'' At that point, Harris shot back, ''The only jerk around here is the president of the ball club.''

In late July, two weeks after the American League won the first night All-Star game in history which was played at Shibe Park, with the Phillies in sixth place, Cox surprised everyone by announcing that Harris had been fired and that pitcher Freddie Fitzsimmons had been obtained from Brooklyn to become the new manager. The players were up in arms over the firing and considered striking in protest until Harris talked them out of it before a game in St. Louis. When Harris returned to Philadelphia and held a news conference, he mentioned that Cox bet on games the Phillies played. That created a stir, since Baseball Commissioner Landis had strict rules about gambling, and a hearing was held. Before Landis made a ruling, Cox wrote him that he was resigning and made a farewell speech on the radio. Later, he tried to retract the resignation, but Landis barred Cox from baseball for life.

Starting Phillies pitcher Hugh Mulcahy (left) stands with Boston Bees starter Jim Turner before the Bees opener in 1939.

Bobby Bragan, who for three years held down the shortstop
position for the Phillies, slides safely into third base in an
early season game against the Brooklyn Dodgers in May,
1941.

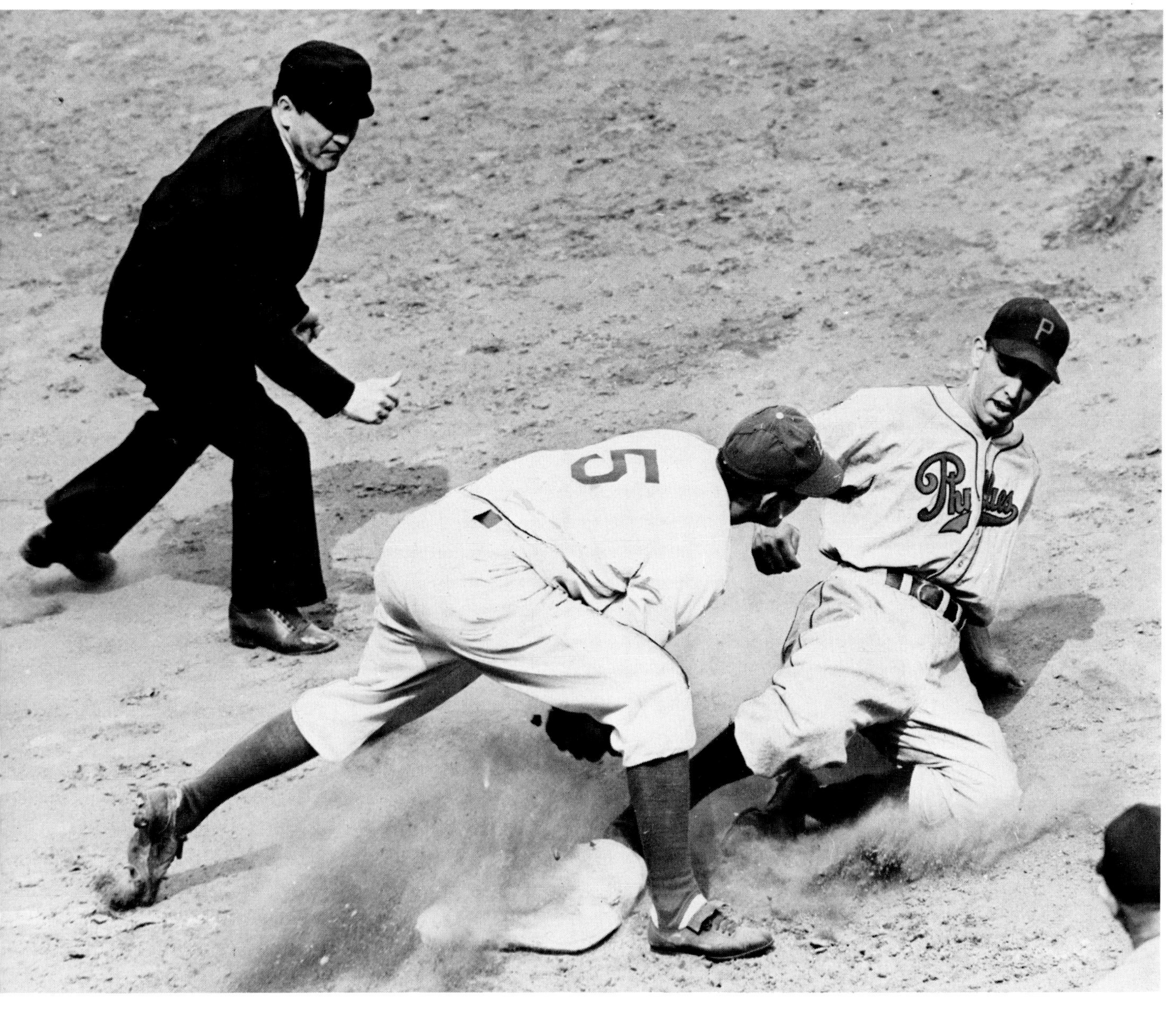

Bucky Harris gets ready to sign the papers that would
make him manager of the Philadelphia Phillies in 1943,
after his term with the Washington Senators. At left is the
club's owner, W.D. Cox, and Chuck Klein, player-coach
of the Phillies, is at right. Harris managed only that one
year, but went on to be selected to the Hall of Fame in
1975. Owner Cox was barred from organized baseball for
betting on games and Klein was voted into the Hall of
Fame as one of the Phillies great players of the late 1920s
and early 30s. He received the honor in 1980.

Baseball commissioner Judge Landis (left) decreed that the
ban on former Phillies president Bill Cox (right) from
holding any office in organized baseball was still valid.
Cox, entangled in baseball wagers in 1943, had asserted
through his lawyer, Lloyd Paul Stryker (center), that the
admission of wagers were part of a trap to test the loyalty
of some Phillies employees. While unfortunate, the
incident opened the way for the Carpenter family's
acquisition of the team.

Ellsworth "Babe" Dahlgren who played only the 1943 season with the Phillies is shown sliding into third base with a triple in a game against the New York Giants. The relay throw pulled Giants third baseman Buster Maynard off the bag as umpire Ralph Pinelli comes over to call the play.

When Bob Carpenter became president of the Phillies in
November 1943, he was 28 years old — the youngest club
president in the history of major league baseball. Despite
his youth, he had a clear vision of what it would take to
build a winner. The plan he worked out with general
manager Herb Pennock bore fruit in 1950. Carpenter served
as president until November 22, 1972 — one day short of
29 years — when he was succeeded by his son, R.R.M.
Carpenter, III.

Chapter Six

CARPENTER TO THE RESCUE

As it turned out, the ban on William Cox was a fortunate development for the Phillies. In short order, the club was sold to Robert R.M. Carpenter, a wealthy duPont Corporation executive who wanted the team for his son, Robert, Jr. The sale for $400,000 was consummated on November 23, 1943, and young Carpenter was installed as the club president. His first move was to hire Herb Pennock, the former great pitcher who was a personal friend of the family. At the time, Pennock was running the Boston Red Sox farm system. Carpenter, who entered the Army shortly after taking over the club, and Pennock agreed that money would be spent to obtain whatever players might be available to improve the club immediately but that the long-range plan would be to build through the farm system. Carpenter, who had been an athlete at Duke University and who had been involved promoting boxing in Delaware and in the operation of the Wilmington team of the Interstate League, gave Pennock a free hand and the necessary funds to get the job done. Both understood that time would be required. The Phillies again finished last in 1944 under Manager Fred Fitzsimmons and again in 1945 under Fitzsimmons and Ben Chapman, a former teammate of Pennock's on the New York Yankees in the early 1930s. Chapman took over the club after the Phillies managed to win only 17 of its first 67 games. Biggest name on the team was Jimmie Foxx, who had gained fame as a slugger with the Athletics and Red Sox. He was playing his last season at the age of 37 as a part-time infielder and pitcher. The only player on that team who was to remain when the club landed on top was Andy Seminick, a catcher who had joined the Phillies late in the 1943 season.

With the end of the war, baseball drew big crowds in 1946, and the Phillies were no exception. Chapman made the Phillies a popular team with his insistence on all-out hustle. Although the club was made up for the most part of veterans on the way down — first baseman Frank McCormick, third baseman Jim Tabor and pitcher Schoolboy Rowe — they moved up to fifth place in their best showing since 1932. The fans, encouraged by the new operation and the team's improvement, set a club record for attendance at home of 1,045,247, more than double the old record set in 1916. In addition to Seminick, the Phillies had another young regular that year who was to help the club win the pennant in 1950. He was outfielder Del Ennis, signed out of Philadelphia's Olney High School in 1943, who hammered 17 home runs and batted .313 to finish fourth in the league in his rookie season of 1946. He was the team's leading run producer and slugger for the next decade.

In 1947 the Phillies fell back to seventh place despite having the league batting champion in center fielder Harry Walker, who had been obtained in an early-season trade with the St. Louis Cardinals. Walker, who later managed in the National League for almost nine years, batted .363 that season and earned the nickname of Harry The Hat for his custom of fiddling with his

The Hamner brothers. Granville "Granny" Hamner (left) and Garvin (right) both with the Phillies in 1945, are shown. Granny went on to turn in solid performances at shortstop and second base from 1948 through 1957, but brother "Garv" was with the team only in 1945.

cap between almost every pitch. The club's best pitcher that year was 38-year-old Dutch Leonard, a knuckleballing right-hander who had been purchased from Washington the previous December and who won 17 games while posting a 2.68 earned run average in his first season with the Phillies.

Before the start of spring training in 1948, the Phillies' rebuilding program suffered a major setback when Herb Pennock, while attending the major league meetings in New York City, suffered a cerebral hemorrhage and died on January 30, just 11 days before his 54th birthday. Carpenter, who had worked closely with Pennock since leaving the service, took over the major operating role and handled the general manager's duties for the next six years. The 1948 season saw several new faces, including rookie center

Twice in the team's history management has attempted to give the Phillies a new image with a new game. The first was in 1909 when Horace Fogel dubbed them the Live Wires. Then in 1944 and 1945 they were called the Blue Jays. Neither name stuck. This pin is a souvenir of the latter effort.

The first female baseball scout belonged to the Phillies. Edith Houghton, 33, an ex-Wave and former star player with girls' teams, started out in the early part of 1946 to seek out talented rookies for the club.

General manager Herb Pennock (left) and team manager Ben Chapman wear smiles coming out of the dugout in June 1946. That year the team finished fifth, a long way from the cellar that it had been occupying for so long.

fielder Richie Ashburn, join the Phillies, but the club struggled. Carpenter was not happy with Chapman, who had received some unfavorable publicity over his riding of Jackie Robinson the year before. He decided to make a change after the All-Star Game break in mid-July. He fired Chapman, named Coach Dusty Cookie interim manager, and 10 days later announced that his new manager would be Eddie Sawyer, a former outfielder who had been hired by Pennock away from the New York Yankees and who had been managing in the Phillies farm system, this season at Toronto, the top club in the system.

Sawyer was an intelligent man who had taught at his alma mater, Ithaca College, in the off-season. He had used a fatherly approach with his young minor leaguers, but he could be tough when necessary, and he had the respect of those who played for him. He spent the rest of the 1948 season learning his players and the league, and the Phillies finished a distant sixth. By the following spring, however, Sawyer was ready to help the club move toward the top.

The money the Phillies had been spending so liberally to sign top prospects was beginning to pay off by 1949. In addition to Seminick, Ennis and Ashburn, who had batted .333 to finish second in the league and who had led the league in stolen bases with 32 as a rookie in 1948, third baseman Willie Jones, shortstop Granny Hammer and pitchers Curt Simmons and Robin Roberts had graduated to the parent club. Deals helped, too. In May, 1947, the Phillies purchased pitcher Ken Heintzelman from Pittsburgh and in April, 1948, they obtained first baseman-outfielder Dick Sisler from St. Louis. After the 1948 season,

Frank McCormick, one of the veterans who played throughout World War II, takes a cut at the ball in spring practice in 1946. McCormick was the Phillies first baseman for that one year, batting .284.

they got outfielder Bill Nicholson from Chicago in a trade for Harry Walker, who had been beaten out of his job by the swift Ashburn. Two more deals with the Cubs produced pitcher Russ Meyer and first baseman Eddie Waitkus before the 1949 season. Another important addition was pitcher Jim Konstanty, who failed in previous big league trials with Cincinnati and the Boston Braves, but who had pitched well for Sawyer in Toronto after perfecting his control and a palm ball. He had joined the Phillies near the end of the 1948 season.

The Phillies now had the personnel to advance, but it didn't happen right away. In mid-June, 1949, they lost Waitkus, shot by a deranged girl in a Chicago hotel where the club stayed. His loss came just after the club had started to jell and to move into contention. Dick Sisler filled in ably for Waitkus and the Phillies were within five games of first place by the end of June. In July, however, the team began to slip and were in a real rut when Sawyer called a team meeting in mid-August and read the riot act, threatening changes if the players didn't pay more attention to their play on the field.

Immediately after the meeting with Sawyer, the Phillies swept a three-game series at Brooklyn, came home and played well, and from then until the end of the season they won consistently to finish in third place in their best performance since 1917. Ken Heintzelman and Meyer, who put together a late-season, eight-game winning streak, each won 17 games; the developing Roberts won 15, Hank Borowy added 12 and Jim Konstanty was developing into a relief ace. Del Ennis, who had slipped below .300 in his

The 1946 climb out of the cellar brought fans back to the ballpark to watch the likes of these men. Left to right: pitcher Charley Ripple, catcher Andy Seminick and pitcher Lyn "Schoolboy" Rowe.

Harry "The Hat" Walker (right) was knocking the cover off the ball in 1947 as Phils center fielder. He is shown in May of that year with first baseman Howie Schultz when his average was .400. He ended the year with a .363 average to lead the league. His nickname came because he fiddled with his hat between nearly every pitch.

Young pitching star Curt Simmons signs with the Phillies in 1947 as his father (center) and general manager Herb Pennock of the Phillies watch. Pennock was brought to the Phillies from the Red Sox by club president Robert Carpenter, Jr., whose father bought the Phils in 1943. Young Carpenter and Pennock agreed that money would be spent immediately for good players, but that the long-range goal was to build the team through the farm system. Young Simmons was one of the best catches for the team.

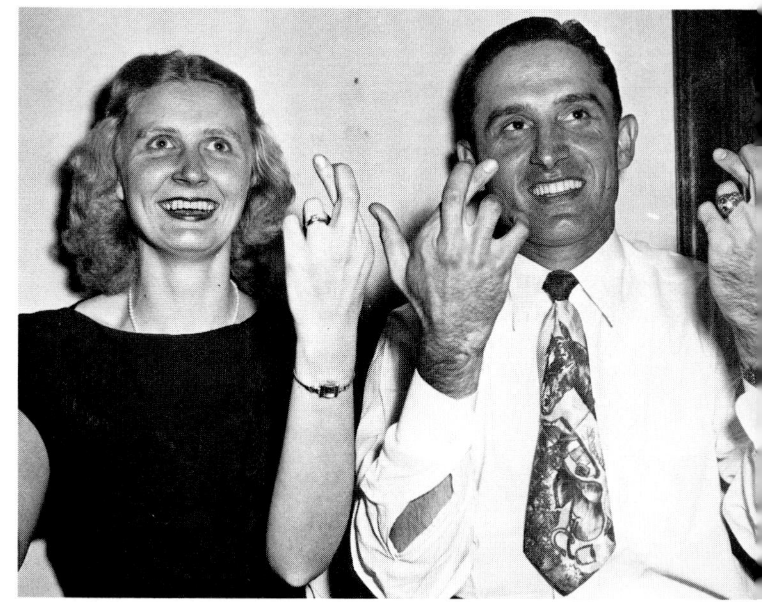

Emil Verban, Phillies second baseman, and his wife hope for good things at the 1947 All-Star game. The Verbans had narrowly escaped injury in a train collision in Chicago and Verban was scheduled for the starting lineup the next day in the All-Star game at Wrigley Field. The crossed fingers were to insure that he suffered no further mishap.

Home-run record-setters (left to right) Schoolboy Rowe, Andy Seminick, Del Ennis and Willie Jones combined to hit five homers in the eighth inning of the June 2, 1949, game against the Cincinnati Reds. The feat tied the record set by the New York Giants in 1939. Seminick hit two round-trippers in the inning, equalling the major league record. The Phils won the game, 12-3.

sophomore season, bounced back to hit .302, with 25 home runs and 110 runs batted in, fifth best in the league.

After their fast finish the year before, there was optimism when the Phillies assembled at their spring training base in Clearwater, Florida, in 1950, but few outsiders thought the club had any reasonable chance to win the pennant. The Brooklyn Dodgers were regarded as the team to beat. St. Louis and Boston were picked by most to finish ahead of the Phillies, who were nicknamed the Whiz Kids because of their tender youth — the average age being only 26. Pitching was the team's strength. Robin Roberts, who had come off the campus of Michigan State to make the grade after less than half a season in the minors, won 20 games for the first time, and Curt Simmons, a highly sought prize when he was a schoolboy in Egypt, Pennsylvania, suddenly developed into a reliable starter, winning 17 games despite missing parts of the season because of National Guard duty. The 17-game winners of 1949, Russ Meyer and Ken Heintzelman, slumped to just nine and three

Granny Hamner, shortstop for the Phils in 1949, kicks the bag for an out on the Dodgers Gil Hodges and fires to Eddie Waitkus at first to complete the double play in this early season game.

Eddie Waitkus recovers in a Chicago hospital after being shot in a hotel where the team was staying during the 1949 season. Waitkus' loss from the lineup came just when the Phillies were beginning to jell. Dick Sisler subbed the rest of the season and Waitkus returned the next year to help the "Whiz Kids" to the pennant.

Dick Sisler stretches at first base as Rocky Nelson of the Cardinals crosses the bag in a 1949 game. Sisler, obtained from the Cards in April 1948, filled in at first base after Eddie Waitkus was injured in a shooting incident in a Chicago hotel.

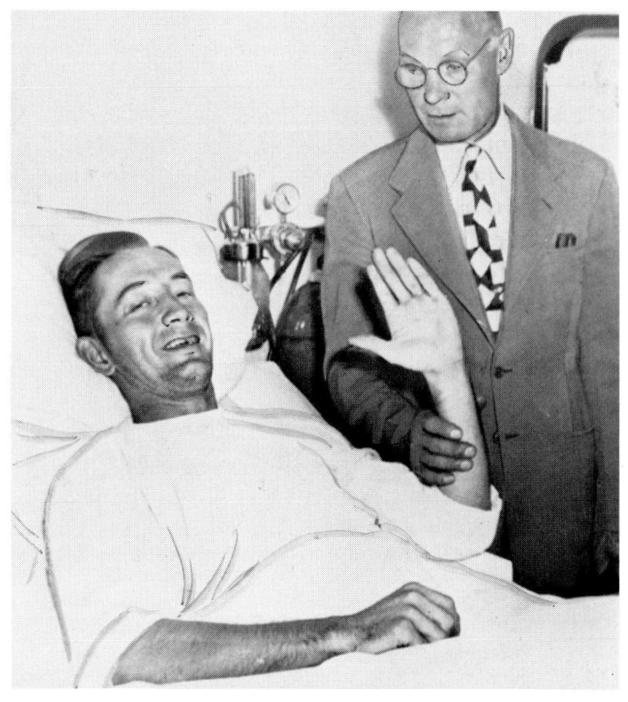

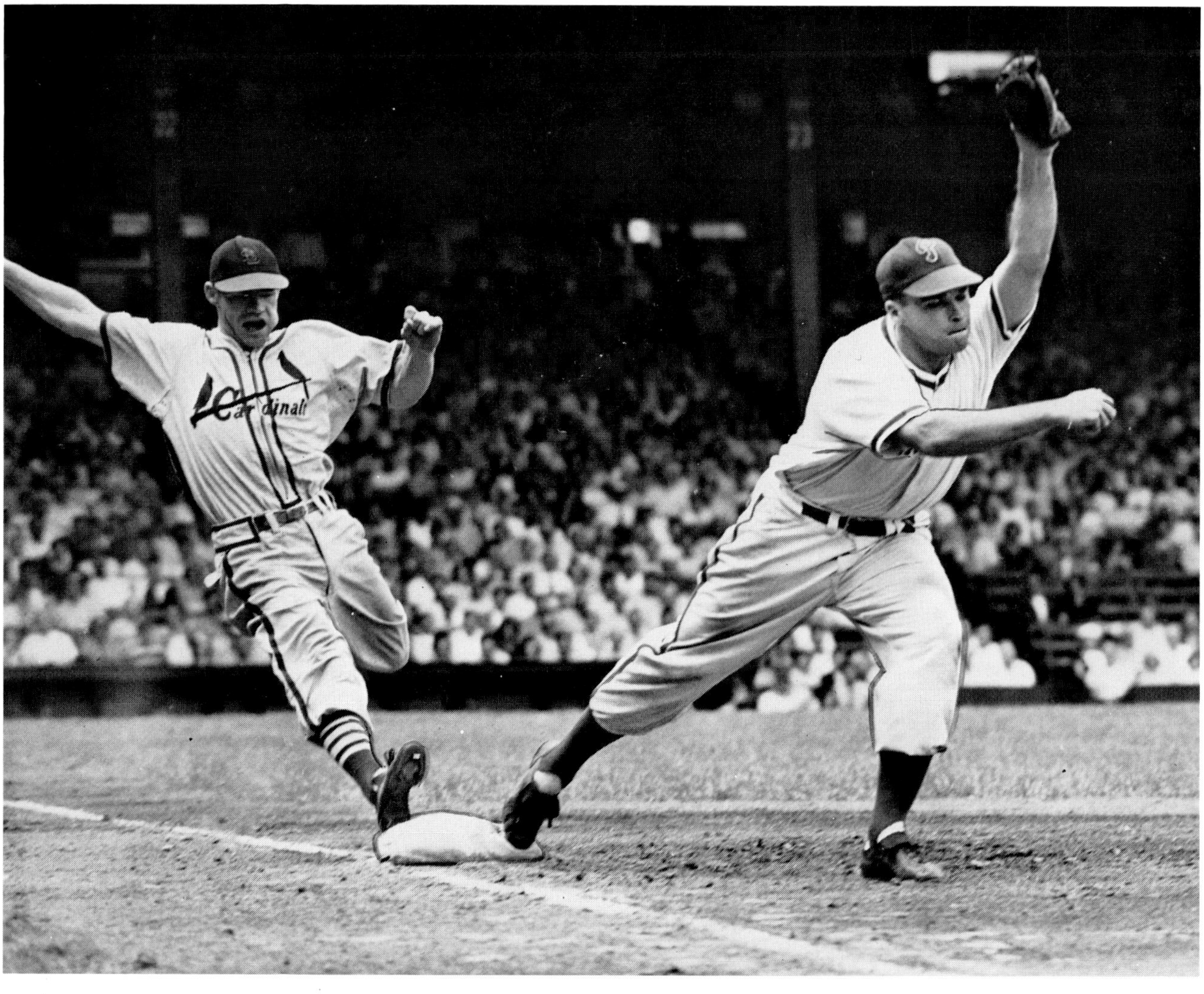

victories respectively, but two rookie right-handers, Bob Miller and Bubba Church, combined to win 19 games and Jim Konstanty was a magician coming out of the bullpen.

Konstanty set two major league records by appearing in 74 games and finishing 62 of them. He won 16 games, lost nine and saved 22 others. Time after time, the bespectacled right-hander came in from the bullpen to stop a rally with an assortment of junk pitches. His work was so outstanding he was singularly honored as the first relief pitcher ever to win the Most Valuable Player Award.

Eddie Waitkus worked hard with trainer Frank Wiechec in the off-season and came back to play first base in his usual smooth manner and batted .284 as the club's leadoff batter. Dick Sisler was switched to left field and enjoyed the best season of his career, hitting .296 with 13 homers and 83 runs batted in. The club's two .300 hitters, Richie Ashburn and Del Ennis, filled the other two outfield spots. Ennis was the offensive leader, batting .311, hitting 31 homers and batting in 126 runs. Ashburn, who led the league in putouts while playing between the not too swift Sisler and Ennis, batted .303 and led the league with 14 triples. With Waitkus in the infield were Mike Goliat, a third baseman converted into a second baseman who never played regularly in the major leagues after this season; strong-armed shortstop Granny Hamner, who knocked in 82 runs, and third baseman Willie Jones, who was second on the club in homers with 25 and in runs batted in with 88. Andy Seminick, who did most of the catching, batted .288 and hit 24 homers. None of the reserves batted over .250.

The Phillies won only two of their first seven games but managed to break even in April and had a 16-9 record in May. None of the other clubs got away to a fast start and the four picked to finish in the first division were all closely

Willie Jones, third baseman, accepts the congratulations of (right to left) the team bat boy, coach Dusty Cooke, and second baseman Mike Goliat after hitting a home run in the eighth inning of a 1949 Phils-Dodgers game which the Phils won, 5-4.

Jim Konstanty, the peerless reliever. Konstanty worked magic coming out of the bullpen in 1950 to turn the Phils into pennant-winners. During that season he appeared in 74 games, finishing 62 of them. His record of 16 wins, nine losses, and 22 saves earned for him the Most Valuable Player Award, the first bestowed on a relief pitcher.

There was good reason for manager Eddie Sawyer to flash a smile in May of 1950 at Pittsburgh. Willie Jones (left) had belted a seventh-inning pitch for a three-run homer and Robin Roberts (right) had posted his fourth win of the season, 3-2, as the Phillies began their race for the flag.

bunched for the first half of the season, so
closely that Brooklyn was in fourth place on July
17 but was only one game from the top. A week
later St. Louis led but that July 25 the Phillies
began a 16-game home stand with a doubleheader
shutout of the Chicago Cubs and went on to take
the lead with 12 victories in the 16 games. The
Phillies, who had led twice for a week in May,
led by three and one-half games at the end of
July, by six games at the end of August and by
seven when they began a home stand against the
New York Giants on Labor Day. Suddenly,
things changed. The Giants shut out the Phillies
twice on the holiday. Brooklyn won the next
three games at Shibe Park to slice the lead to four
and one-half games. The Phillies halted that
slump to lead by seven and one-half games on
September 15 and, with only 11 days remaining
in the season, still led by seven and one-half
games five days later.

The loss of Curt Simmons, whose Guard unit
had been called to active duty on September 10,
began to be felt, along with injuries to Bob
Miller and Bubba Church. Miller, who had won
his first eight decisions, had been sidelined with a
back injury; an eye injury, suffered when he was
hit by a batted ball, sidelined Bubba Church for
more than a week in mid-September. Neither
Miller nor Church was of much help down the
stretch.

With nine days left, the Phillies' seven-game
lead began to melt. The Dodgers swept a
two-game series. After the Phillies managed to
win two out of three from Boston, New York
won two successive doubleheaders from the
frontrunners. Brooklyn won four of six games
from Boston and the Phillies moved into Ebbets
Field for the final two games of the season with
their once comfortable lead down to two games.

When the Dodgers beat the Phillies, 7-3, on
Saturday, the margin was a single game, and the
Phillies called on Robin Roberts to make his third
start in five days in the season finale on Sunday,
October 1. He was opposed by Brooklyn star
Don Newcombe, like Roberts a 19-game winner
going into the game. Robbie was making his
sixth try for his 20th victory. Willie Jones singled
home a run for the Phillies in the sixth inning,
but Pee Wee Reese tied the score in the home
half with a freak home run. His drive to right hit
the screen, dropped onto a ledge and stayed there
as Reese circled the bases. The score was still
1-1 when Cal Abrams opened the last of the ninth
with Brooklyn's second walk of the game. Reese
failed trying to bunt, but singled to left. Duke

**Granny Hamner comes away from second base after making
the throw on a double play in June of the year that became
known as the year of the "Whiz Kids."**

Four of the "Whiz Kids" whose pitching put the Phils in first-place on July 27, 1950 (left to right with manager Eddie Sawyer): Bubba Church, 4 wins; Robin Roberts, 12 wins; Bob Miller, 8 wins; and Curt Simmons, who gained his 14th victory on that date by beating the Chicago Cubs, 13-3.

The Boys of a Super Summer. September 16, 1950, and the Phils were 7½ games ahead of the Dodgers in the final drive for the pennant with only 14 games left to play. In this photo are (left to right) manager Eddie Sawyer, Eddie Waitkus, Mike Goliat, Granny Hamner, Willie Jones, Andy Seminick, Del Ennis, Richie Ashburn, and Jack Mayo.

Snider followed with a line single to center and third-base coach Milt Stock inexplicably waved Abrams home. The Dodger outfielder, a poor runner, was an easy out when center fielder Richie Ashburn threw home and catcher Stan Lopata, who had replaced Andy Seminick, applied the tag. The runners moved up on the throw home and Roberts walked Jackie Robinson intentionally to load the bases, then retired Carl Furillo on a foul pop outside first base and Gil Hodges on a fly to right to end the inning.

In the 10th inning, Roberts started the game-wining rally with a ground single to center. Eddie Waitkus followed with a looping single to center. Ashburn's bunt forced Roberts at third and brought up Dick Sisler, who had already singled three times off Newcombe. With the count one ball and two strikes, Newcombe made a pitch on the outside corner and the lefthanded-hitting Sisler lined a three-run homer into the left field stands for the game-winner.

Roberts retired the Dodgers in order and the Phillies had won, 4-1, to clinch their second pennant, and their first in 35 years. It took almost as long before the Phillies won their third.

The pennant victory set off a wild celebration in Philadelphia and it had barely subsided before the Phillies went out to face the New York Yankees in the World Series. Their pitching rotation was a shambles, and the 1950 Phillies fared even worse than did the 1915 club. The Yankees won four straight games, although the Phillies continued the pattern set 35 years before, losing the first three games by a single run, the first two at Shibe Park.

In the opener on Wednesday, October 4, Manager Sawyer sprang a surprise by nominating Jim Konstanty, his brilliant relief pitcher, for the starting assignment, although the right-hander had pitched 133 straight games in relief for the Phillies without starting a game since being called up from Toronto at the end of the 1948 season.

The Whiz Kids of the outfield. From left: Dick Sisler in left field, Richie Ashburn in center, and Del Ennis in right. These three accounted for some great hitting and fielding for the 1950 Phillies, who won the pennant against the heavily favored Dodgers.

Konstanty pitched brilliantly, but not as well as Yankee right-hander Vic Raschi, who allowed just two hits and won, 1-0. The game's only run was scored in the fourth inning by third baseman Bobby Brown, a left-handed hitter who doubled inside third base and came around to score on fly balls to center and left by Hank Bauer and Jerry Coleman.

In the second game the next day, Robin Roberts and Allie Reynolds matched pitch for pitch through nine innings, each yielding a run. Joe DiMaggio, who had popped out all four times at the plate previously in this game and hadn't hit a ball out of the infield in the two games, led off the 10th inning with a line drive home run into the upper left field stands. Despite a leadoff walk in the home 10th, the Phillies, who had three doubles and a triple among their seven hits, couldn't score. The 2-1 victory sent the Yankees back to Yankee Stadium with a commanding advantage.

The Phillies had their best chance to end their World Series losing streak in the third game on Friday, October 7. Left-hander Ken Heintzelman opposed Yankee southpaw Eddie Lopat. The Phillies led for the only time in the Series when Granny Hamner and Mike Goliat singled around a sacrifice in the seventh to put the visitors in front, 2-1. The Yankees had scored in the third on a walk, stolen base and Jerry Coleman's single, and the Phillies had tied the score in the sixth when Del Ennis doubled and scored on Dick Sisler's single. With two out in the home eighth, however, Heintzelman suddenly lost his control and walked three straight batters. Jim Konstanty was called in from the bullpen to face Bobby Brown, a pinch-hitter for Hank Bauer. Konstanty appeared to have ended the threat when he got the left-handed batter to hit a routine grounder to shortstop. Granny Hamner fumbled the ball for his only error of the Series, and the score was tied. Konstanty was lifted for a

The grounds crew re-dos the infield at Connie Mack stadium in preparation for the Phillies first World Series appearance in 35 years.

The player who capped the pennant. It was down to the wire with the Dodgers on October 1, 1950. If the Phils won, the pennant was theirs. And here's the man who won it: Dick Sisler. The Phillies had played with their heart during 1950. In this sequence of photos, Sisler slides into second base as Jackie Robinson of the Dodgers waits for the throw at the start of what could have been a double play. Sisler comes into second in a cloud of dust, taking Robinson down with him and spoiling the play at first on teammate Del Ennis. Although Sisler was out on this play, he hit a home run with two men on base in the 10th inning to win the game for the Phillies, 4-1, and to bring the pennant to Philadelphia.

Welcome home, champ. That's what the mass of Phillies are screaming to teammate Dick Sisler (No. 8) as he crosses home plate after hitting a 10th-inning home run to beat the Brooklyn Dodgers, 4-1, and win the National League pennant for the Philadelphia Phillies in 1950.

pinch-hitter and replaced on the mound by Russ Meyer.

In the 10th, the New Yorkers scored when sub second baseman Jimmy Bloodworth misplayed two ground balls into singles and Jerry Coleman dropped a fly-ball single into left center to win the game, 3-2.

The World Series ended the next day. The Yankees chased rookie Bob Miller and scored two runs in the first inning, and added three more in the sixth off Konstanty, who relieved in the first and was making his third appearance in four days. The Phillies struggled for eight innings against Whitey Ford, the left-handed Yankee rookie, but rallied in the ninth to put their first two runners on base. Two outs later, Seminick hit a fly ball to left that Gene Woodling dropped for a two-run error. When Mike Goliat singled to bring the tying run to the plate in the person of pinch-hitter Stan Lopata, Allie Reynolds replaced Ford and blazed three fast balls past the big right-hander to seal the 5-2 victory and end the Series.

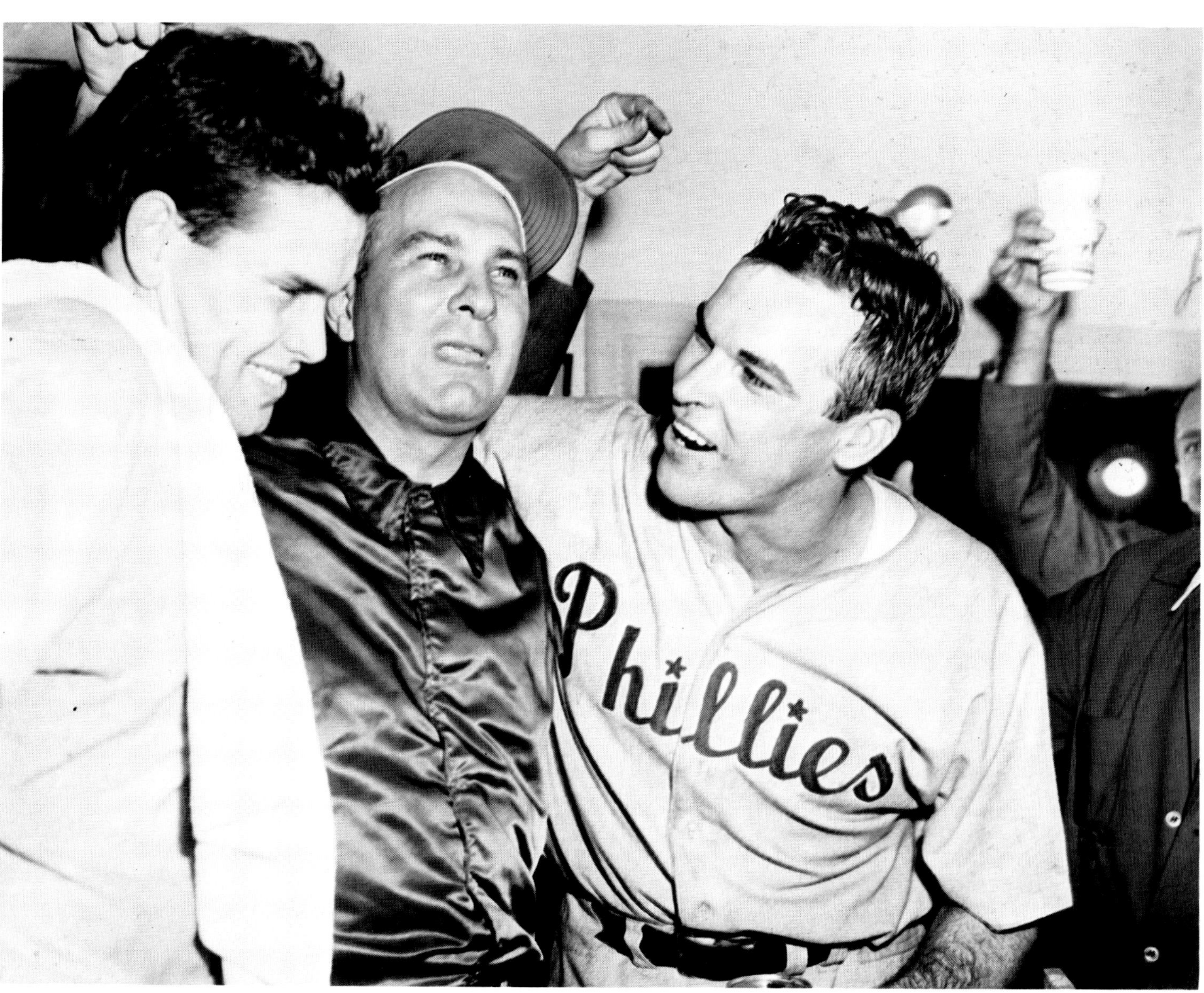

Manager Eddie Sawyer tried to smile through his tears of joy as the two heroes of the Whiz Kids, Robin Roberts (left) and Dick Sisler (right), give him a victory hug. Sisler's 10th-inning homer and Roberts' five-hitter brought the flag to the Phils on October 1, 1950.

Fans gathered at the train station to celebrate with their
pennant-winning Phils when the team arrived in
Philadelphia after their win over the Dodgers at Ebbets
Field.

The Official Whiz Kids Team Picture, 1950. Seated (left to right): Jimmy Bloodworth, Blix Donnelly, Richie Ashburn, Putsy Caballero, coach Benny Bengough, manager Eddie Sawyer, coach Cy Perkins, coach Dusty Cooke, Del Ennis, Dick Sisler, and Willie "Puddin' Head" Jones. Middle row (left to right): trainer Frank Wiechec, Bubba Church, Bob Miller, Ken Heintzelman, Ken Silvestri, Stan Lopata, Stan Hollmig, Robin Roberts, Dick Whitman, Russ Meyer, Granny Hamner, Jocko Thompson, and traveling secretary Frank Powell. Back row (left to right): Ken Johnson, Steve Ridzik, Eddie Waitkus, Milo Candini, Jack Mayo, Jim Konstanty, Andy Seminick, Mike Goliat, Jack Brittin, Paul Stuffel, and coach Maje McDonnell. The bat boy is Kenny Bush.

The Phillies victory over Brooklyn for the National League
crown was bigger news in Philadelphia than the Korean
War. Small wonder, given the 35-year wait between
pennants.

Phils Win National League Pennant

LATEST SPORTS

**Two Full Pages of Pictures
And Stories of the Phillies
Today on Pages 34 and 35**

Fans Dance in Streets As Town Goes Wild Over Phillies' Victory

The Fighting Phillies brought Philadelphia its first National League pennant in 35 years at exactly 4:39 o'clock yesterday afternoon. Ten seconds later the city went wild.

There was dancing in the streets and spontaneous celebrations from one city line to the other. The lid was off and joy was unrestrained as thousands jammed toward the North Philadelphia station to welcome their baseball heroes coming in from New York aboard the Pennsylvania Railroad at 7 o'clock express from New York.

Congratulatory messages began to flood the Phillies' Shibe Park offices while Bob Carpenter's pennant winners were still in their working clothes over in Brooklyn's Ebbets Field.

SISLER THRILLS MACK

"I extend my sincere congratulations to Eddie Sawyer and his boys on winning the National League pennant," said Connie Mack, whose Athletics finished in the cellar of the American League.

"They won the biggest game of the season, the one in the clutch that counted more than any other, and truly lived up to their name as the Fighting Phillies. Young Roberts pitched a remarkable game and

World Series Guide Free With Inquirer

The Philadelphia Inquirer will include the World Series Guide, a 16-page magazine supplement, with all editions of the issues of Wednesday, Oct. 4 — opening day of the World Series.

The separate guide will cover fully—in pictures and stories—the background of the Phillies and their Series opponent, with final batting, fielding and pitching averages for the 1950 season.

Individual stories on Eddie Sawyer, Jim Konstanty, Del Ennis and a special story on the 1915 pennant-winning Phillies by Stan Baumgarntner will be included in the magazine, in addition to famous World Series plays and infamous boners. Complete World Series score cards also will appear in the World Series

Brooks Bow On Homer By Sisler

By STAN BAUMGARTNER
Inquirer Sports Reporter

BROOKLYN, Oct. 1. — Dick Sisler's mighty blast into the left-field stands for a home run with two on base and one out in the 10th inning carried the Fightin' Phillies to their first National League championship in 35 years today.

Tonight, amid publication over their spectacular victory, the Whiz Kids looked forward toward the World Series and Wednesday's first game against the New York Yankees, American League title-winners, at Shibe Park.

ROBERTS HURLS TRIUMPH

Sisler's dramatic clout, combined with sensational pitching by Robin Roberts and a thrilling ninth-inning throw to the plate by Richie Ashburn, gave the Whiz Kids a 4-1 triumph over Brooklyn's battling Dodgers in the final game of the regular season before 35,073 the year's largest crowd at Ebbets Field.

It was a tingling climax to one of the finest contests of 1950—a game that bristled with great fielding plays, magnificent pitching in the pinches by both Roberts and Don Newcombe, the Brooks' fireballing ace. It was one of the great battles of baseball history, and drama rode on each pitch. A pennant hinged on the outcome, and everyone—fans, players and press—shared in the terrific tension.

DAD SEE SISLER'S HOMER

And one of the happiest of all in the great victory was a gray-haired, slightly built man who sat on the Brooklyn side of the field in a box adjacent to the Dodger dugout—George Sisler, Dick's dad and one of baseball's immortal first basemen. As the Phillies hugged and kissed the leftfielder as he romped over the plate, his dad stood and tossed his hat in the air.

Roberts hurled a brilliant five-hitter as he finally won No. 20 and became the first Phil hurler to win 20 games since Grover Cleveland Alexander captured 30 games in 1917. And even more, Robin opened the winning rally with a single over second. Eddie Waitkus followed with a looping single to center to send Robbie to second.

THROW CUTS OFF RUN IN 9TH

Ashburn, whose great peg to the plate had cut off what would have been the Dodgers' winning run in the ninth, then laid down a bunt, but forced Roberts at third.

Then Sisler stepped to the plate. In his four previous trips, Dick had

Konstanty, Ennis to Cover Series

A great galaxy of baseball experts—writers, reporters and columnists—will bring readers of The Inquirer every detail of the World Series between the National League pennant winners, the Phillies, and the American League champions, the New York Yankees.

And with these stories and articles, written by trained Inquirer staff men, readers also will be given the inside facts about the Phillies and the World Series games by two of the greatest players on the championship team:

Jim Konstanty, the incomparable relief pitcher who has become one of baseball's greatest names by his terrific hurling this season, and

Del Ennis, the sluging outfielder, who leads the league as a "clutch" hitter and whose bat is feared by every pitcher in both leagues.

"Professor Jim" and "Big Slug" will write daily articles exclusively for readers of The Inquirer dealing particularly with pitching and batting—their own methods and ideas and the problems they face when on the mound or at the plate.

Pre-game articles by these two outstanding players appear today on Page 33.

This is the first championship series for the Phillies since 1915 and The Inquirer has planned all-out coverage so that its readers will not miss any feature or thrill.

A corps of trained photographers will be on hand under the direction of Frank Johnston, chief photographer, to give readers action shots on the field and views of the crowds and notables.

Stan Baumgartner, a member of the Phillies' 1915 World Series team, and a staff writer who has covered the Phils' games for many years, will be on hand to present the game facts not only from a sportswrtier's viewpoint, but also with his own invaluable baseball background to add the expert touch.

Art Morrow, for many years a follower of the American League clubs and who has made a particular study of the pennant contenders in that league, will specialize during the series on the Phils' opponents.

S. O. (Sog) Grauley, Inquirer sports editor and a veteran of more than 50 years experience in baseball coverage, will write articles comparing the present day game with those of the past. 'Sog" has seen all of the greats of baseball in action and is the only writer who could give first-hand comparisons.

Henry Littlehales and Allen Lewis, two sportswriters who have followed baseball, will produce important highlight material along with other members of the department.

The crowd reactions and views of the famous and near-famous who will sit in boxes and bleachers will be covered by Allie Crawford, and a staff of local news reporters.

Ivan H. (Cy) Peterman, news columnist, and John Webster, sports columnist, will give daily columns on the series and its ramifications.

John M Cummings, political columnist, has promised to take his "Uncle Dominick" along and get an eye-witness account of the doings.

In addition to the staff writers and the special articles by Jim Konstanty and Del Ennis, the full facilities of the writers from the Associated Press, the United Press, the International News Service, the New York Herald Tribune Service and the Chicago Tribune-New York Daily News Service will be available.

Before and during the series the baseball news will be covered thoroughly and accurately by The Inquirer.

<table><tr><td>SPORTS
COMPLETE
FINANCIAL</td><td>The Philadelphia Inquirer
PUBLIC LEDGER
An Independent Newspaper for All the People</td><td>STAR
EDITION</td></tr></table>

August Circulation: Daily 695,343; Sunday, 1,110,258   MONDAY MORNING, OCTOBER 2, 1950   122nd Year   FIVE CENTS
Copyright, 1950, by Triangle Publications Inc, Vol. 243, No. 94

S. Koreans Cross Border

Patrols Advance 7 Miles Unopposed

Reds' Reply Awaited To Surrender Demand

TOKYO, Oct. 2 (Monday) (AP).—South Korean troops plunged north across the 38th Parallel in force Sunday while Gen. Douglas MacArthur awaited response from the North Korean Communist regime to an ultimatum for surrender or "early and total defeat." The historic crossing was made on the extreme east coast in the vicinity of burning Yangyang

World Series
1950
FIRST GAME
1950 WORLD SERIES
Phillies 1950 WORLD SERIES
GRANDSTAND
OFFICIAL PROGRAM
FIFTY CENTS

Eddie Waitkus drives a deep fly in the 1950 World Series. The Yankee catcher is Yogi Berra.

Manager Eddie Sawyer playfully hugs New York Yankees pilot Casey Stengel before the opening game of the 1950 World Series which went to the Yankees, 1-0.

The first pitch of the first game of the 1950 Series. Jim Konstanty throws to Yankees leadoff batter Gene Woodling. Catcher is Andy Seminick and the umpire is Jocko Conlan. This pitch to Woodling was a ball. Konstanty gave up five hits and one run before being replaced by a pinch hitter in the eighth inning.

Jim Konstanty (right) got the call to start for the Phils in the first game of the 1950 World Series. Konstanty had pitched 133 straight games in relief, but hadn't started a game since being called up from Toronto in 1948. He allowed only one run, but that was enough and the Yanks took the first game, 1-0. With Konstanty just before the start of the game are other Phillies pitchers (left to right) Russ Meyer, Robin Roberts, Ken Heintzelman, and Bubba Church.

Third baseman Mike Goliat scores the Phillies first run in the 1950 World Series after tagging up at third on Richie Ashburn's deep fly. It came in the fifth inning of the second game at Shibe Park after Goliat led off with a single and advanced to third on a single by Eddie Waitkus.

Inches made the difference between victory and defeat for the Phillies. In the top photo, Granny Hamner slides home in the seventh inning of the third game of the Series for a 2-1 lead over the Yankees. Teammate Ed Waitkus (No. 4) gives the slide sign as Yankees pitcher Ed Lopat backs up the plate. The umpire is Dusty Boggess. In the lower pictures, Hamner slides into home plate (picture 1) in the top of the ninth inning on a ground ball by pinch-hitter Dick Whitman to Jerry Coleman, but this time Yogi Berra successfully makes the tag. The Yankees scored once in the bottom of the ninth to win, 3-2.

Sometimes a hero, sometimes a goat. Such is baseball. Dick Sisler had brought the 1950 pennant to Philadelphia with a 10th-inning home run against the Brooklyn Dodgers on October 1, 1950. Here, Sisler strikes out, in the bottom of the 10th inning in the second game of the World Series to end the game, won by the Yankees, 2-1.

Robin Roberts, the Phillies great pitcher of the late 1940s and the decade of the 1950s, came off the campus of Michigan State and ended up in the Hall of Fame in 1976. He put together one of the most impressive pitching records in baseball history, winning 20 or more games for six consecutive years. His 10th-inning leadoff single in the 1950 pennant-clinching game with Brooklyn demonstrated that he was an all-around ball player; in that game he made his third start in five days and he retired the Dodgers in order in the bottom of the 10th for the second pennant in Phillies history.

Chapter Seven

GREAT EXPECTATION

In spite of the disappointing performance in the 1950 World Series, Phillies fans believed their Whiz Kids were starting a dynasty that well might produce several more pennants before the stars of that team passed their peaks. They never came close. In the next 13 years, the best the Phillies could do was a tie for third place in 1953, a whopping 22 games in back of Brooklyn, and a fourth-place finish in 1952, nine and one-half games behind the Dodgers. The attendance, which hit a record 1,217,035 in 1950, fell with the club and didn't reach the million mark again until 1957. In 1951 the Phillies limped home fifth as both Andy Seminick and Del Ennis had below-par years and the loss of Curt Simmons was still being felt on the pitching staff. Richie Ashburn had a big year, leading the league with 221 hits and hitting .344 to finish runner-up in the batting race. Willie Jones led the club with 81 runs batted in and 22 homers. Robin Roberts paced the mound staff with 21 victories and Bubba Church won 15, but no other pitcher won more than eight.

Owner Bob Carpenter was reluctant to break up the 1950 club and tried to patch and fill where the club needed help. But he did trade Andy Seminick and Dick Sisler to Cincinnati after the 1951 season for second baseman Connie Ryan, catcher Smoky Burgess and pitcher Howard Fox, and later dealt away pitcher Bubba Church. The Phillies got away poorly in 1952 and lost 11 of 13 games in late May and early June. By late June, Carpenter decided that Sawyer, who had cracked the whip hard with an austerity program in spring training after the poor 1951 showing, would have to be replaced.

On June 17 Carpenter reluctantly fired Sawyer with the Phillies owning a 28-35 record. He named Steve O'Neill the new manager. O'Neill had managed for more than a decade in the American League and was scouting for the Boston Red Sox. He took off all the restrictions and the Phillies responded by winning 59 games and losing 32 the remainder of that season. Robin Roberts enjoyed a banner year in 1952, winning 28 games and losing only seven while pitching 30 complete games. Curt Simmons returned to win 14 games, Karl Drews also won 14 and Russ Meyer captured 13 as the Phillies led the league

with a team earned run average of 3.07. But no regular hit .300 and the club home run total was only one more than the league low.

The Phillies got away fast in 1953, winning nine of their first 11 games, but a five-game losing streak in late May and a freak injury to Simmons, who lost part of his left big toe to his power mower on June 4 and was out of action for a month, slowed down the club. Still, the left-hander won 16 games, seven fewer than staff leader Roberts and two more than Jim Konstanty, who was used 19 times as a starter. Richie Ashburn, with a league-leading 205 hits and a .330 average, was the only .300 hitter, but Del Ennis hit 29 home runs and batted in 125 runs.

The National League Pennant (top, right) waves over the Phillies home, Shibe Park, in 1951 for the first time in 35 years. The Phillies won the flag in 1950, helped greatly by pitcher Jim Konstanty, who won 16 games and was voted the league's Most Valuable Player.

Granny Hamner, shifted to second base when shortstop Ted Kazanski was promoted at mid-season from the minors, hit 21 homers and batted in 92 runs.

Increasingly in recent years, owner Bob Carpenter heard criticism of his failure to hire a trained baseball executive to run the club, and in mid-April 1954 he signed H. Roy Hamey to a five-year contract as the club's general manager. Hamey had held several executive posts in baseball: American Association president, general manager of the Pittsburgh Pirates and various jobs with the New York Yankees over a lengthy period. During Hamey's tenure, the Phillies finished fourth twice, fifth twice and eighth in his final season after which he returned to the Yankees. Four managers were fired in that time, starting with Steve O'Neill in a surprise move on July 15, 1954, with the Phillies in third place with a 40-37 record. Terry Moore, former star outfielder with the St. Louis Cardinals, succeeded O'Neill but the Phillies finished under the .500 mark and in fourth place under Moore, who was then released. Roberts continued to be a big winner that year with 23 victories. Simmons won 14 and two newcomers, Murry Dickson, obtained in a trade with Pittsburgh, and Herman Wehmeier, who was purchased in June from Cincinnati, each won 10. Catcher Smoky Burgess batted .368 in his third season with the Phillies, Ashburn batted .313 and Ennis had his usual production of 119 runs batted in and 25 homers.

The 1954 season was the last one the Phillies shared a park with the Athletics, who moved to Kansas City upon the club's sale by the Mack family. On December 10 Carpenter bought Connie Mack Stadium, the name of which had been changed from Shibe Park prior to the 1953 season, for $1,657,000. The Phillies played there until they moved into Veterans Stadium in 1971, although Carpenter sold the old park in 1961 and leased it back from the owners.

These three Phillies almost single-handedly shoved Brooklyn into a league tie with their archrivals, the Giants, down the home stretch of the pennant race in 1951. Left to right: Andy Seminick who hit a home run to tie the game at 3-3, Willie Jones who drove in the winning run, and fleet-footed Richie Ashburn who raced home to score the winning run.

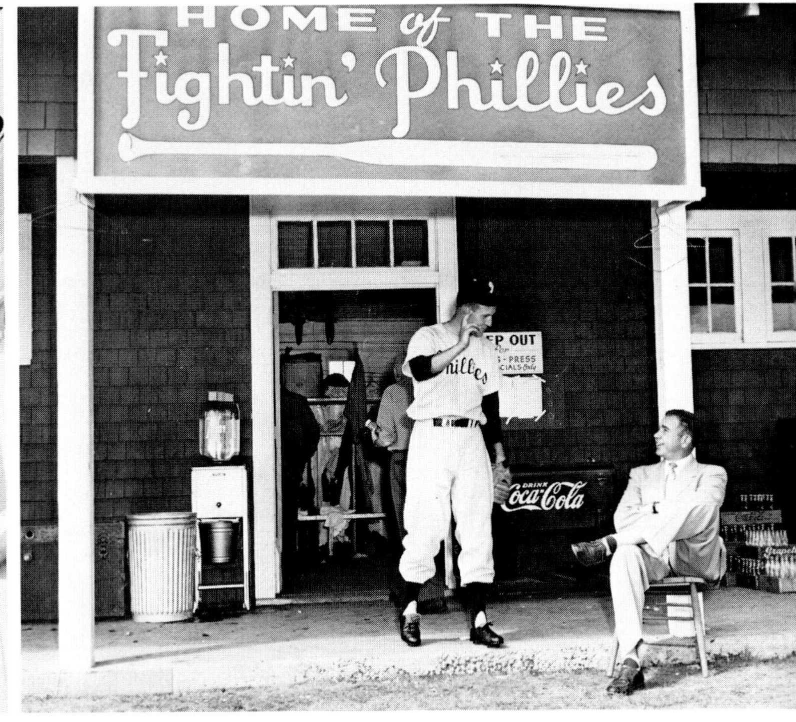

The Phillies opened 1952 spring practice in Clearwater, Florida, still smarting from their poor showing in the 1951 pennant race. Despite the somber atmosphere, there was still time for jokes: pitcher Russ Meyer looks at Bill Nicholson's uniform which teammates had nailed to the ceiling of the locker room. Hold-out third baseman Willie Jones is shown taking it easy outside the clubhouse as Meyer heads to the practice field.

Curt Simmons' (right) great career was interrupted by military service in 1950 just as it was getting started. Here he is welcomed back by owner Robert Carpenter and manager Eddie Sawyer after his discharge in 1952.

By the 1950s the fields and the scenery had improved
markedly for the clubs when they went to spring training.
Here a well-kept infield waits for the Phillies to finish
pre-practice warmups.

The deadly pitching duo of Robin Roberts (left) and Curt
Simmons brought the Phillies their second pennant in 1950.
Both pitchers were the result of the Phillies liberal
spending of money to attract good players. Roberts had
come to the Phillies after less than half a season in the
minors and Simmons was a highly sought-after prize when
he was a young player in Egypt, Pennsylvania. Roberts
posted 20 wins in 1950 and Simmons won 17 before being
called to active duty with the National Guard in September.

Hamey dipped into the New York Yankee farm system after the 1954 season to replace Terry Moore and selected Mayo Smith, who had played the outfield for the Athletics in 1945 and who had managed the Birmingham club in the Southern Association for the past two years. Smith, who had been managing for the Yankees for six years, was an unknown to the players on the Phillies. This problem was compounded when the club went into a losing streak on April 30 that lasted through 13 games. That skid dropped the bottom out of the season, although, helped by an 11-game winning streak in July, the Phillies won 40 of their last 70 games and managed to finish fourth again. Richie Ashburn, the swift towhead from Nebraska, won the first of his two National League batting titles with a .338 average and Del Ennis had a typical year with 120 runs batted in and 29 home runs. Andy Seminick came back from Cincinnati at the end of April, but his skills were eroding and this was his final season as a first-string catcher. Robin Roberts was easily the best of the pitchers, leading the league in wins with 23 and in complete games with 26, but the staff's No. 2 man, Murry Dickson, won only 12.

Spring woes again plagued the club in 1956 as

It was practice that made for perfection with Phillies star hitter Del Ennis. Here he takes his cuts during batting practice in Shibe Park. Smoky Burgess, who was the Phillies mainstay at catcher from 1952-1954, is behind the plate.

the Phillies lost 10 games in a row and 15 of their first 20 games. However, they rebounded to win more games than they lost in June, July and August and finished fifth with six fewer victories than in 1955. Partly because he was having physical problems and partly because he gave up a still-standing major league record total of 46 home runs, Robin Roberts failed for the first time since 1949 to win at least 20 games. A loss to the New York Giants on the final day of the season gave him a 19-18 record. Curt Simmons made a comeback to win 15 games, and left-hander Harvey Haddix, obtained from Pittsburgh in a May trade, won 12. Stan Lopata emerged as the first-string catcher and hit 32 home runs to lead the team and tied Del Ennis for the runs batted in lead with 95.

It now was obvious that the Phillies needed

The lights are on at Connie Mack Stadium for a Phillies night game. President Carpenter bought Connie Mack Stadium, the name of which had been changed from Shibe Park before the 1953 season, for $1,675,000. The purchase came after the Athletics, with whom the Phils shared the park, went to Kansas City when sold by the Mack family. The Phillies remained in Connie Mack Stadium until 1971, when they moved to Veterans Stadium.

new blood if they were to improve. They got it in 1957 when they made a surprising showing in the first half of the season before sinking to fifth again with a .500 record. A poor season by Roberts, who won 10 games and lost 22, kept the Phillies from a first-division finish. Four rookies played key roles on this club. Jack Sanford, a hard-throwing right-hander, came out of the service the previous September and won 19 games in his first full season and led the league in strikeouts. Dick Farrell, another right-hander who threw hard, became a star in relief with 10 victories and 10 saves. First baseman Ed Bouchee batted .293, hit 17 homers and led the team in runs batted in with 76. Left fielder Harry Anderson, another service returnee, hit 17 homers and batted in 61 runs. Rip Repulski, obtained from St. Louis in a trade for Del Ennis, led the

team in homers with 20, and Stan Lopata's total dipped to 18. A shortstop problem was solved when an April trade with Brooklyn produced Chico Fernandez of Cuba, the first black ever to play for the Phillies.

Although the hitting left a lot to be desired — the Phillies scored more runs than only last-place Pittsburgh — they stayed with the leaders in a five-team race through the early months; only four games separated the first five at the end of July. The Phillies won 12 of their first 14 games in July to take over first place on July 15 after sweeping a Sunday doubleheader from St. Louis the day before and then beating the Cards again on Monday night behind Sanford. The Phillies were the fifth of the five contenders to hold the lead; it was their first time in first place after May since 1950. The stay lasted two days. The

Del Ennis (left) holds a placard announcing his 1,000th RBI with the Phillies in 1955, only the second player in team history to manage the feat. Ennis ended his Phillies career with 1,124 RBIs, second only to Ed Delahanty with 1,286. Helping Ennis celebrate his 1,000th in the locker room are (left to right) Bobby Morgan, Herm Wehmeier, and Jim Greengrass.

eventual champion Milwaukee Braves began a three-game series sweep of the Phillies the next night. A 9-19 record in August killed any hopes for a Phillies miracle.

An anticipated comeback by Robin Roberts, the spring showing of rookie right-hander Ray Semproch and the addition of slugging outfielder Wally Post, who came from Cincinnati in a trade for pitcher Harvey Haddix, were causes for optimism when the 1958 season began. Unfortunately, the team followed pretty much the same pattern as the year before. The Phillies were in contention at mid-season, then played badly in the final 80 games and finished last, although no big league tailender ever won more games than the 69 they captured. A seven-game winning streak just before the All-Star Game moved the Phillies to within two and one-half games of the lead and they were still only that far back after

winning two of their first three games on the road through July 12. The next day the Phillies lost a doubleheader in Chicago to start a seven-game losing streak with the first four all by one run. By the time they returned home from the West Coast after an exhibition game on July 21 in Minneapolis, they trailed by eight and one-half games. The next day Mayo Smith was fired and Eddie Sawyer, who had suffered the same fate six years before under similar circumstances, was named manager. The Phillies won their first two games under Sawyer, but only 28 of the final 69 to finish eighth, 23 games back.

Robin Roberts bounced back to win 17 games that season. Ray Semproch won 13, but only two after July 12. Jack Sanford, the 19-game winner the year before, won only 10. Dick Farrell, almost unhittable through the All-Star Game when he struck out four of the seven American

Granny Hamner hits the bag to force Jackie Robinson out at second base and throws to first base for the double play in the 1956 game against the Dodgers. Hamner started his career with the Phillies in 1944 and saw action for a number of years at shortstop before spending his final season as a Phillies regular at second base in 1957. Phillies second baseman Ted Kazanski is at right.

Chico Fernandez proved to be a solution to the Phillies problems at shortstop as the 1957 season began. Fernandez, a Cuban, was obtained in an April trade with Brooklyn. He played regularly for two years, batting .262 in his first year and dropping to .230 in 1958. He is acknowledged as the first non-Caucasian to play for the Phillies.

League batters he faced, was a complete bust the last half of the season. He had a 6-2 record, nine saves and a 1.13 earned run average through the club's first 76 games, but finished with an 8-9 log, 11 saves and an ERA of 3.35. Ed Bouchee, arrested on a morals charge in January, did not return to baseball until July 1 and both he and Wally Post were disappointments, too. Harry Anderson, who played left field and first base, hit 23 homers, knocked in 97 runs and batted .301. Richie Ashburn won his second batting crown with a great finish, getting 16 hits in his last 27 times at bat in the final week to beat out Willie Mays on the final day. Veteran first baseman-outfielder Dave Philley excelled as a pinch-hitter, leading the league with 18 pinch-hits, including a record eighth in succession on the season's last day.

A deadly combination of hitting power and solid pitching accounted for an 8-3 Phillies win over the Los Angeles Dodgers in May 1958. Catcher Stan Lopata (left) and third baseman Granny Hamner (right) accounted for seven RBIs and rookie pitcher Ray Semproch won his third game and held the Dodgers to five hits. Lopata hit a homer and a single and Hamner slammed a bases-loaded triple and the 100th home run of his career.

Robin Roberts welcomes new manager Gene Mauch to the Phillies locker room. As it turned out, this photo could well represent the end of one era and the beginning of another in Phillies history: Roberts and the 1950s and Mauch and the 1960s.

Chapter Eight

NEW LEADERSHIP

Roy Hamey's contract was due to expire early in 1959 and the veteran executive hadn't been able to make the Phillies bona fide contenders during his regime. Owner Bob Carpenter was determined to build a winner. When he learned that veteran executive John Quinn would be interested, he went after the man who had put together the 1948 pennant-winning Boston Braves by trades, who had guided the Milwaukee Braves clubs that had won in 1957 and 1958 and had lost in a playoff in 1959 through building with young farm system products. A long-term contract and a sizeable salary increase brought Quinn to Philadelphia in January, 1959, while Hamey returned to New York where he realized his dream of becoming general manager of the Yankees after the 1960 season.

Quinn's first objective was to upgrade the scouting staff and try to sign the best available talent for the future. Revamping the major league club proved more difficult than improving the farm system. The Phillies finished last again in 1959. They didn't have a .300 hitter, finished last in runs scored, batting and slugging averages, and in fielding, too. Their only winning pitcher was Gene Conley, the pro basketball center obtained March 31 from Milwaukee in Quinn's first trade. Quinn made many minor deals trying to improve the club but his next major trade was one of his best ever. He swapped infielder-outfielder Gene Freese, who played third base most of 1959 and blossomed into a home run hitter with 23, to the Chicago White Sox for outfielder John Callison, a highly prized prospect who had suffered a knee injury in winter ball. Quinn also traded Richie Ashburn to the Chicago Cubs in a deal that did not pan out so well.

Eddie Sawyer had been selected by Carpenter to be the manager before Quinn arrived in Philadelphia, and the two did not always see eye to eye in 1959 or in the spring of 1960. When the Phillies returned home after losing their 1960 opener at Cincinnati, Sawyer resigned in a move that startled almost everyone, although no one detailed the reasons for the move. With a chance to pick his own man, Quinn selected one he'd had his eye on for some time. His name was Gene Mauch, whom Quinn had recommended for the job of player-manager of Atlanta in the

Southern Association back in 1953. Mauch guided the Crackers to a third-place finish that year but decided he wasn't ready to manage, and went back to being a full-time infielder, eventually reaching the major leagues again at the end of the 1956 season as a second baseman with the Boston Red Sox. After the 1957 season, the Red Sox named him manager of their American Association farm club at Minneapolis, where he finished third and second in his two years there and was about to begin his third when Quinn hired him. Mauch, a fiery type with a great baseball mind, may not have realized right away how really talent-poor the Phillies were. He found out in a hurry, however, and then played a major role with Quinn in the decisions that rebuilt the team into a contender. That took time, and not every decision was correct.

John Quinn took over as Phillies general manager in 1959 after developing the championship Braves. In five years he built the Phillies into a pennant contender.

Mauch quickly decided that the club's prime needs were a catcher and a second baseman, and the Phillies traded first baseman Ed Bouchee and pitcher Don Cardwell to the Chicago Cubs on May 13 for catcher Cal Neeman and second baseman Tony Taylor, who was to become one of the most popular athletes in any sport ever in Philadelphia. Two days before that deal, the Phillies handed pitcher Curt Simmons his unconditional release, and that proved to be a major mistake. The left-hander signed with the St. Louis Cardinals and enjoyed several productive seasons, helping the Redbirds win the 1964 pennant with 18 victories. In mid-June the Phillies sent outfielders Wally Post and Harry Anderson to Cincinnati for young outfielder Tony Gonzalez, who played for the Phillies for nine seasons and averaged .295. The Cuban didn't play regularly in his rookie season in 1960, although Tony Taylor did and hit .287, but the only member of the Phillies with more than 10

home runs or 40 runs batted in that year was rookie first baseman Frank (Pancho) Herrera. He batted .281 with 17 homers and 71 RBIs, but he also struck out a record 136 times. On the pitching staff, the only starter to win more than eight games was the fading Robin Roberts, who won 12 while losing 16. Farrell made a comeback to win 10 games in relief and save 11 more, and rookie Art Mahaffey came up from the minors in late July to win seven of 10 decisions. With only 59 victories the Phillies finished eighth for the third straight year but the worst was yet to come.

In 1961, the Phillies won only 47 games, finished last and suffered the ignominy of the longest losing streak in modern major league history. Starting on July 29 with a 4-3 loss at home to San Francisco, the Phillies lost 23 straight games before right-hander John Buzhardt, an 18-game loser this season who had dropped 11 straight decisions the year before, won the second

Gene Conley (left) wears one of two different kinds of uniforms in 1959 as he gives some pitching tips to Ted Lepcio who was traded to the Phillies by the Detroit Tigers. Conley, a pitching ace with the Phillies, played basketball for the Boston Celtics during baseball's offseason.

Tall talent was what Phillies pitching coach Tom Ferrick (kneeling) had when spring training got under way in Clearwater, Florida, in 1959. These four hurlers averaged 6 feet, 4 inches. From left: Don Cardwell out of Winston-Salem, North Carolina; Dick Farrell of Brookline, Massachusetts; Jim Hearn of Atlanta, Georgia; and Dallas Green of Wilmington, Delaware. That's right, Dallas Green, the same individual who guided the 1980 Phillies to the World Championship.

Richie Ashburn (right) set a torrid pace at the close of the 1958 season to hit .350, beating out Willie Mays for the batting title on the last day. Here he hands a load of bats to new Phillies Valmy Thomas and Ruben Gomez at the start of spring training in 1959. By this time Ashburn had established himself as one of the game's greats. He led the league twice in average and triples and three times in hits while compiling a lifetime average of .311. Ashburn is the all-time Phillies leader in games, at bats, and hits. Small wonder his number "1" joins Robin Roberts' as the only Phillies numbers to be retired.

game of an August 20 doubleheader at Milwaukee, ending a 10-game winning streak by the Braves. When the Phillies flew home that Sunday night, several hundred fans were waiting at the airport to greet them. Peering through a window while waiting to deplane, Frank Sullivan, a tall veteran pitcher with a large sense of humor, yelled to his teammates, ''Get off in twos and threes so they can't get us all with one burst. They're selling rocks at a dollar a pail.''

Despite their poor record, the groundwork was being laid for a contender and Mauch maintained that the record losing streak had a positive effect. ''Instead of thinking of themselves as ex-Reds, ex-Cubs, ex-Braves or whatever, the losing streak brought them together, and made them think of themselves as Phillies,'' he said.

That year the Phillies obtained third baseman Charley Smith and outfielder Don Demeter from the Los Angeles Dodgers in a May 4 trade for pitcher Dick Farrell. They got left-handed slugger

An unusual shot of Tony Gonzalez as he takes a cut at the ball. Gonzalez was a fine hitter during his nine seasons with the Phils, hitting .300 or more in three seasons.

Wes Covington in a July 2 deal with the Kansas City A's. Clay Dalrymple, who had had troubles at the start of his rookie season the year before, was developing into an excellent catcher, and Ruben Amaro had come up the year before to provide classy defense at shortstop. That 1961 season was the final one for Robin Roberts with the Phillies. The eventual Hall of Famer won only one of 11 decisions to give him 234 victories, most in club history. He was sold after the season to the New York Yankees.

Before the 1962 season, the Phillies traded for first baseman Roy Sievers and pitcher Cal McLish. Both veterans played a part in the team's first winning record, 81-80, in nine years, although the club finished seventh in the newly expanded 10-team league. Art Mahaffey won 19 games and McLish and young left-hander Chris Short, slowly developing into a winner, won 11 apiece. Jack Baldschun in his sophomore season blossomed into a standout relief pitcher. Don Demeter, converted into a third baseman, and outfielders John Callison and Tony Gonzalez all hit .300 or better and these three, along with first baseman Sievers, each hit at least 20 home runs. Rookie Bobby Wine, a strong-armed infielder, came up this season to divide the shortstop job with Amaro.

Mauch was convinced the Phillies were ready to move into the first division and he drove his players hard the next season. The Phillies, however, started so slowly that on June 23, when they lost a Polo Grounds doubleheader to the New York Mets, they fell nine games under .500 and were mired in seventh place. But they went to Pittsburgh and swept a three-game series, and won 56 of their last 91 games. Only the pennant-winning Los Angeles Dodgers won more over that stretch. The Phillies finished fourth with 87 victories, one game in back of the San Francisco Giants and they did it despite a string of injuries. Pitcher Dennis Bennett, who had won nine games as a rookie in 1962, suffered a broken ankle in an auto accident in January in Puerto Rico where he was playing winter ball. He didn't pitch until June 25, but still won nine games. A sore shoulder and an ankle injury prevented Mahaffey from winning more than seven games. Rookie Ray Culp, although injured part of the season, won 14 games, one more than McLish. Power was supplied by Callison, who hit 26 home runs; by Demeter, who hit 22 while playing mostly in the outfield, and by Sievers, who hit 19. Demeter led the club with 83 runs batted in, one more than Sievers, and five more

Clay Dalrymple had some troubles at the start of his rookie season in 1960, but began to put his catching talents together in the losing season of 1961. He was not a strong hitter, but his work behind the plate, catching such pitchers as Jim Bunning and Chris Short, made him a key player during much of the 1960s.

Don Demeter was converted from an outfielder to third baseman before the 1962 season and contributed a mighty bat to the club's greatly improved showing in an expanded 10-team league. Demeter hit over .300. He, outfielders John Callison and Tony Gonzalez, and first baseman Roy Sievers all hit at least 20 home runs. The following year he was back in the outfield for most of the season and still powerful at the plate, hitting 22 homers.

Ray Culp unleashes a pitch to a New York Yankees batter in an exhibition game in 1963, the year that Culp won 14 games as a rookie for the Phillies and pitched in the All-Star game.

Believing he had the makings of a fine team, Gene Mauch (center) drove his team hard down the stretch in 1963, closing with a three-game sweep of the Dodgers. The heroes on the last day were Bobby Wine (left), who tied the game with a homer in the seventh, and Johnny Callison (right), who drove in the winning run. The win enabled the Phillies to edge the Reds for fourth place and a share of the World Series money — two good reasons for all the smiles.

than Callison.

The Phillies played their last 11 games on the road in 1963, and they had won two in New York and broken even in two at Houston when they faced the Astros for the final time on September 22. Chris Short carried a 1-0 lead into the ninth when the Astros rallied to tie the score. Then, with two out and John Klippstein on the mound in relief, Joe Morgan, just recalled from Durham of the Carolina League, grounded a single through the right side to win the game.

Mauch, for whom temper displays after tough defeats were fairly commonplace, was incensed at being beaten by the 5-foot, 7-inch Morgan, "who looks like a Little Leaguer." When the manager entered the clubhouse at Colt Stadium, the first thing he saw was the usual after-game food spread laid out by the clubhouse man. Mauch overturned the tables, and food and the barbecue sauce made a mess of the clothes hanging in the lockers of Covington and Gonzalez. Determined that the Phillies wouldn't let down in the final week, Mauch drove the club to two victories in three games in San Francisco and a sweep of the three-game series in Los Angeles. That enabled them to beat out Cincinnati for fourth place by one game.

When the Phillies traded Don Demeter and pitcher Jack Hamilton to the Detroit Tigers the following December 4 in exchange for pitcher Jim Bunning and catcher Gus Triandos, they were ready to compete for the 1964 pennant.

Art Mahaffey gets his No. 28 uniform from clubhouse man C.A. Pressnell while fellow pitcher Chris Short looks on as the Phillies ready for 1964 spring training at Clearwater, Florida. Mahaffey went on to win 12 games that season, Short won 17, and the Phils ended in a tie for second place in the league.

They had the best defense in the league at shortstop with Amaro and Wine, and Cookie Rojas had developed into a capable player who was at home at second base or in the outfield. Mauch, who liked to maneuver, used Rojas in all nine positions by the Cuban's fifth season with the Phillies in 1967 when he pitched a scoreless inning. At third base, replacing the veteran Don Hoak who had filled the spot in 1963, Mauch decided to convert rookie outfielder Richie Allen. Although the muscular all-around athlete had begun his pro career as an infielder, he had never before played third. Despite making 41 errors, most by any player in either league in 1964, Allen made up for his defensive shortcomings with his bat. He hit .318 to lead the club, and was the runnerup in both home runs with 29 and runs batted in with 91. The homer and RBI leader was John Callison, who had developed into a standout right fielder with an accurate arm. He tied for third in the league with 31 homers and was fifth in runs batted in with 104. First base was a trouble spot until the veteran Frank Thomas was obtained from the New York Mets on August 7. He played well until he suffered a broken thumb sliding on September 8, an injury that forced him to miss 17 days and prevented him from ever regaining his batting stroke.

The dedicated Jim Bunning was the pitching staff leader Mauch knew he would be: he won 19 games. Chris Short won 17, Dennis Bennett and Art Mahaffey 12 apiece, and Ray Culp won eight despite some arm trouble. Jack Baldschun and veteran Ed Roebuck, purchased in April from Washington, were an effective relief duo, combining to win 11 games and save 33.

Richie Allen was as tough at the negotiating table and off the field as he was at the plate. He increasingly became embroiled in controversy during his first tenure with the Phillies from 1963-1969. Allen's batting ability, nonetheless, was revered and he was selected for three straight years, 1965-67, to the All-Star team.

Richie Allen was an outfielder who was converted in his rookie year with the Phillies to a third baseman in 1964 by manager Mauch. Allen had begun his professional career in the infield, but he'd never played third. He made 41 errors in his first year at third base, the most by a player in either league. Despite his weak defense, he was a contributor at the plate, batting .318 to lead the club, and he was runner-up in home runs with 29 and in RBIs with 91.

Richie Allen kicks up a cloud of dust as he slides into second in a game against the San Francisco Giants at Connie Mack Stadium in June 1968.

Just about everything jelled for Mauch and his 1964 team until the final two weeks. They made history in a negative way by blowing the pennant with the biggest collapse at the finish in major league annals. They held a six and one-half game lead with 12 games remaining, but lost 10 straight and finished in a tie for second place with Cincinnati, one game behind St. Louis. The Phillies won their first three games this season and got off in front. They jockeyed with San Francisco for first place much of the early months until they moved into the lead on July 16 and held it until September 27. In all, they led for 134 days, and on August 20 they had their biggest lead, a seven and one-half game margin over San Francisco and Cincinnati and 10 over St. Louis.

At the season's close, Mauch was roundly criticized for his handling of his pitching staff in the closing weeks. First, he started Jim Bunning in Houston on September 16 with only two days of rest instead of his usual three after his ace had pitched 10 tough innings at San Francisco to win his eighth straight game, the longest streak by any Phillies pitcher since 1952. Bunning was chased in the fifth inning of a game the Phillies lost, 6-5, although the Colts had scored a total of only one run in the two previous games of the series. A four-game series at Los Angeles followed and the Phillies gained a split when Bunning won the finale on September 20. That night they returned home with a six and one-half lead that seemed to be safe.

The Phillies' final home stand began with a 1-0 loss to Cincinnati the next night despite the fine pitching of Art Mahaffey. The lone run scored when infielder Chico Ruiz stole home with two out in the sixth inning and slugger Frank Robinson at the plate. That defeat triggered the 10-game losing streak, the Reds beating Chris Short and Dennis Bennett the next two nights to sweep the series. The Milwaukee Braves were next and they beat Bunning, 5-3, the next night. Mauch then pitched Short with two days' rest in the Friday night game. The left-hander lasted until the eighth but the Braves won in the 12th,

7-5, despite two-run homers by John Callison in the eighth and by Richie Allen in the 10th, both tying the score.

The bitterest loss in the slump came the next afternoon when Mahaffey went into the eighth inning with a 4-2 lead. The Braves scored once in that inning when southpaw Bobby Shantz relieved, and then banged the veteran for three runs in the ninth on Rico Carty's bases-loaded triple to center field. The seventh straight defeat came the next afternoon in the season's final home game despite three home runs by Johnny Callison. Bunning, pitching again with only two days between starts, was routed in the six-run Milwaukee fourth-inning rally, being charged with seven runs, most given up by him in any game that season. Callison hit solo home runs in the sixth and eighth innings and a two-run homer in the ninth, but they went to waste and the

Keeping his eye on the ball. Johnny Callison works on his timing in spring training in 1965. His 31 homers and 104 RBIs helped spark the Phils in the near-miss 1964 campaign. His hard work paid off in 1965 with another 32 home runs and 104 RBIs. Among the Phillies all-time leaders in several hitting categories, Callison was also an excellent outfielder, setting a major league record by leading the league in assists for four consecutive years, 1962-65.

Phillies fell out of first place. They trailed
Cincinnati by one game, with St. Louis another
half game back. By now, the panic was on in
earnest and Mauch again pitched Short without
his regular rest the next night when the Phillies
opened a three-game series in St. Louis. The
left-hander was lifted in the sixth inning in a 5-1
loss to the Cardinals and Bob Gibson. There was
no improvement the next night as the Cardinals
beat sore-armed Dennis Bennett, 4-2, and the
Redbirds completed the series sweep and handed
the Phillies their 10th straight loss on Wednesday
night, September 30. It was an 8-5 game in
which Bunning, pitching again with two days
between starts, was routed in the four-run fourth
inning when the Redbirds took an 8-0 lead.

The 10-game losing streak had seen the Phillies
go from a six and one-half game lead to third
place, two and one-half games behind St. Louis

Jim Bunning put on a Phillies uniform in 1964 after being
traded by the Detroit Tigers and he quickly cloaked himself
in immortality. It was a Sunday afternoon, June 21, at Shea
Stadium and Bunning took the mound against the
hometown Mets. Slowly, inning by inning, the Mets batters
went down without getting on base. Only once, in the fifth
inning on a hard hit ball between first and second, did the
Mets come close to a hit. When it was over, Jim Bunning,
above displaying his form, had pitched a perfect game,
setting down 27 batters in a row. It was the first such
game in the National League since 1880. The Phils won it,
6-0, and Bunning struck out 10 men.

and one and one-half in back of Cincinnati where the Phillies had a night off on Thursday. The Reds beat Pittsburgh that night at home to move to within one-half game of first place and appeared headed for a victory on Friday night. They led the Phillies, 3-0, after seven innings, although they had wasted a chance to take a bigger lead in the fourth because the Phillies executed a triple play on a line drive to left center field. The Phillies, however, rose up in the eighth inning to score four runs and held on to win, 4-3, and snap their slump. St. Louis also lost that night and again on Saturday when the Reds and Phillies were idle, and the season came down to the final game on Sunday with the two leaders in a flat-footed tie, the Phillies one game back, and the league was making plans for a two-team and even a three-team playoff. The Phillies won the last game easily, 10-0, as Jim Bunning pitched a six-hitter and Richie Allen hit two home runs. That tied the Phillies with the Reds, but St. Louis rallied to beat the New York Mets and win the pennant.

Among the highlights of that season, aside from the pennant race, was the All-Star Game played at Shea Stadium when Johnny Callison hit a three-run home run with two out in the ninth inning to give the National League a 7-4 victory. But the most thrilling performance at Shea Stadium that season came on Sunday afternoon, June 21, when Jim Bunning pitched the first complete perfect game in the National League since 1880 as the Phillies won that doubleheader opener, 6-0. The closest the New York Mets came to a hit was with one out in the fifth inning when second baseman Tony Taylor made a diving stop to his left of a hard smash off the bat of Jesse Gonder. The ball bounced away from Taylor a foot or two but the second baseman picked it up and threw to first while on his knees to retire the Mets catcher by more than a stride. Bunning, who struck out 10, was yelling at his mates on the bench in the late innings. The tall right-hander, who had pitched a no-hitter in Detroit back in 1958, was chattering, ''Nine more to go . . . six more . . . three more . . . dive for those balls.'' In the ninth inning, he

retired former Phil Charley Smith on a foul pop behind third, struck out pinch-hitter George Altman, and then ended the game by striking out pinch-hitter John Stephenson with a curve ball.

Despite the bitter disappointment in 1964, general manager John Quinn and manager Gene Mauch felt they had the nucleus of a winner, and needed only a first baseman and more pitching to make another run for the pennant in 1965. Before the year ended, they swapped sore-armed Dennis Bennett to the Boston Red Sox for first baseman Dick Stuart, noted as much for his poor fielding as for his long-distance hitting; they obtained veteran righthander Ray Herbert from the Chicago White Sox, and zany lefthander Bo Belinsky from the Los Angeles Angels, for whom he had pitched a no-hitter in 1962 but had done little else.

The Phillies got away slowly but moved into third place on July 9, just three games off the lead, by winning 11 of 15 games in one stretch.

That was it, however, as they lost eight of their next 10 to fall to fifth place and wound up in sixth, 11½ games behind. Both Stuart and Belinsky were disappointments and the publicity they received upon joining the club did not sit well with some of the players. Stuart hit 28 homers but batted only .234, and Belinsky, hampered by a rib injury, won just four games, one less than Herbert. Bunning won 19 games again and his seven shutouts were the most by a Phillies pitcher since 1917. Chris Short won 18 and had five shutouts, and Ray Culp won 14. The rest of the staff, including the relievers, did poorly. Johnny Callison had another big year with 32 homers and 101 runs batted in, but Allen's home run total fell to 20, although his fielding improved. Cookie Rojas played seven different positions and led the team by batting .303 while playing in 142 games.

One disruptive incident occurred the night of July 3 at a time when the Phillies were moving

John Callison jogs across the plate with the Phillies first run in the second inning against the Chicago Cubs as Cookie Rojas gives him the sign not to slide. Callison was obtained in December, 1959, in a trade with the Chicago White Sox. He batted .300 in 1962. In 1964 and 1965 he hit over 30 home runs and batted in over 100 runs.

up on the leaders. During batting practice, Frank Thomas began needling Richie Allen, and the youngster finally had had enough. He swung and Thomas swung back with his bat, catching Allen on the shoulder. That night the Phillies placed Thomas on waivers, and Mauch forbid Allen to talk to media members about the incident under threat of a heavy fine.

Before the 1966 season, the Phillies made several changes. First, they obtained veteran first baseman Bill White and shortstop Dick Groat from St. Louis, and relief pitcher Darold Knowles from Baltimore, then sent Dick Stuart to the New York Mets. In April they got veteran pitchers Larry Jackson and Bob Buhl in a trade with the Chicago Cubs for three players, including rookie pitcher Ferguson Jenkins. Jenkins became a star and won 20 or more games for the Cubs for six straight seasons. With the exception of Buhl, the newcomers did about as well as was expected for the Phillies, who finished fourth. Just 24 games into the season, the Phillies were seven and one-half games behind, but they moved to within one and one-half games of the top on June 8, then lost 11 of their next 16 and were never in contention the rest of the way, finishing eight games back.

Jim Bunning won 19 games for the third year in a row and Chris Short won 20 for the first time. Jackson won 15 and Knowles won six and saved 13 as the only reliable relief pitcher, but he fell off badly the last half of the season. Richie Allen had a big year, despite missing four weeks with a dislocated shoulder. He hit 40 homers and batted in 110 runs. White hit 22 homers and batted in 103 runs, but right fielder Johnny Callison tailed off badly with only 55 runs batted in and 11 homers.

Chris Short prepares to rifle a pitch to the Cubs Ernie Banks in a 1966 contest. Short had begun to develop as a first-rate pitcher in the early 1960s and won 17 or more games in 1964, 1965, 1966, and 1968.

An off-season Archilles tendon injury made White a liability in 1967. A freak accident on August 24, when Allen put his right hand through the headlight of an automobile he was pushing, ended his season. The Phillies were doomed. Injuries to Short and shortstop Dick Groat helped make the year a disaster. The club started slowly again and, although two eight-game winning streaks in August moved them into second place temporarily, they were still 11 games back at the time and never really in the race. They lost two more games than they won after Allen was injured and wound up in fifth place.

Things went from bad to worse in 1968 when the Phillies finished in a tie for seventh. Gene Mauch was fired and the team's offensive production was its poorest since World War II. Mauch's problems with Allen led to his firing and to the end of the then longest term by any Phillies manager in this century. On April 30 Allen arrived late for a game in New York. At the end of May a groin injury put him out of the lineup and the slugger, now openly defying Mauch and some of his rules, reportedly refused to pinch-hit during a game on the West Coast. On June 8 before a night game in Los Angeles, Mauch declared, ''As long as I'm the manager, Dick Allen will never again wear a Phillies uniform.''

Two days later, Allen met with owner Bob Carpenter after the team's return home and the situation seemed resolved. It wasn't. Between games of a doubleheader the night of June 14, Mauch left to visit his ailing wife in California. The next afternoon it was announced that Mauch had been fired and that Bob Skinner, manager of the team's top farm club in San Diego, had been promoted in his place.

Allen, who played left field this season because of his hand injury the year before, immediately went on a slugging spree, hitting 13 home runs in his first 30 games under Skinner. From July 15 on, however, Allen batted only .210, although he did wind up second in the league in home runs with 33. Allen had little help on offense as Callison, with 14, was the only other player to hit more than nine homers. The .264 batting average Tony Gonzalez compiled led the team. Of the pitchers, left-hander Chris Short, the new staff leader with the trade of Jim Bunning to Pittsburgh the previous December, rebounded to win 19 games, Larry Jackson won 13 and former Pirate Woodie Fryman 12.

Skinner, who bent over backwards in an attempt to get the most out of Allen, failed to last out the 1969 season, and his problems with the slugger were a major reason. First, Allen missed the team plane on May 2 and failed to arrive in St. Louis in time to start either the game on Friday night or on Saturday afternoon. For this he was fined $1,000. Then, on June 24, he did not show up at Shea Stadium for a twilight-night

Phillies first baseman Bill White hits home plate in a dead heat with Pittsburgh Pirates first baseman Dave Roberts in a 1966 game. The Phils won, 7-3, in a game marked by erratic play. In this incident, a throw from Willie Stargell got through catcher Jesse Gonder in the eighth inning to allow White to score. White came from St. Louis, in a trade that included Dick Groat, and he held down first base for three years, hitting a high of .276 in 1966, including 22 home runs and 103 RBIs. An offseason injury in 1967 cut short his potential.

Frank Lucchesi of Foster City, California, and a 19-year manager in the minors tries on a Phils uniform in September 1969 after being named the new manager by president Robert Carpenter. Lucchesi had spent 14 of his minor-league years with Phillies farm teams and he was a popular and enthusiastic manager. But injuries plagued his teams and he lasted only 2½ seasons.

Cookie Rojas adds a stolen base to his performance in a 1968 game against the St. Louis Cardinals. Rojas had developed into a solid second baseman and outfielder by 1964 and, by his fifth year with the Phils, he had been used at all nine positions, pitching a scoreless inning in 1967.

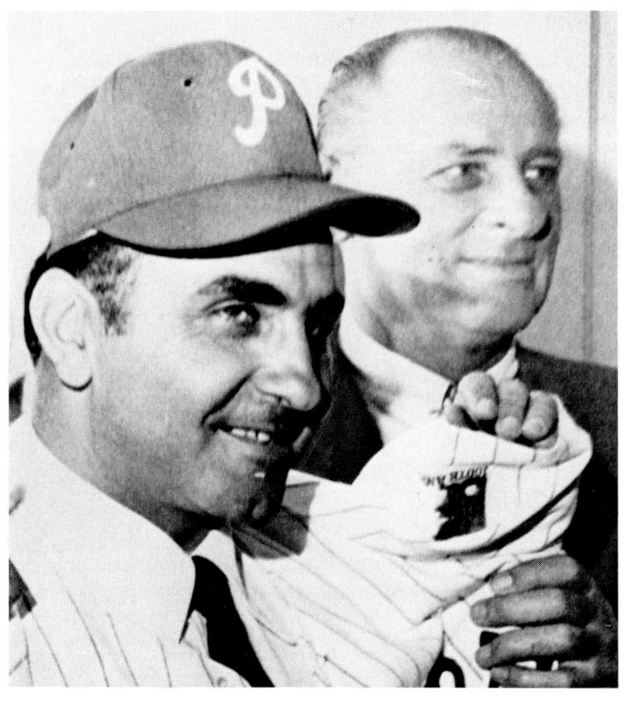

doubleheader with the New York Mets. Skinner suspended him and the suspension lasted until July 20. He didn't play again until July 24 when the Phillies suffered their 17th loss in their last 24 games. Earlier in Allen's absence, the Phillies had won nine straight games, all on the road. The climax came on August 7 when Allen informed his manager he was not going to Reading for the team's scheduled exhibition game. At mid-afternoon, Skinner resigned, claiming that management would not back him up in his handling of the slugger, who was exclusively a first baseman this season. George Myatt, who had been the third-base coach since 1964, managed the team the rest of the season as the Phillies limped home fifth in the first season the major leagues were divided into six-team divisions.

The 1969 Phillies were an improved club on offense despite their poor showing, but the pitching was weak. Allen hit 32 home runs and knocked in 89, and five teammates hit a dozen or more homers. Deron Johnson, picked up from Atlanta, divided his time between the infield and outfield, hit 17 homers and knocked in 80 runs. Rookie center fielder Larry Hisle hit 20 homers, four more than right fielder Johnny Callison. On the pitching staff, a back injury kept Chris Short from winning a game and the only winning starter was young Rick Wise, who won 15 games and lost 13. Left-hander Grant Jackson, in his first year as a regular starter, won 14 but lost 18

Don Money played his first full season with the Phillies in 1969 and remained with the club through 1972. He was one of several promising young players to begin maturing for the Phils during the late 1960s and early 1970s. He played shortstop and third base. Here, he waits for a throw to second base as Willie Mays slides into the bag.

and Woodie Fryman had a 12-15 record.

The Phillies finally decided they had reached the end with Allen after the 1969 season. They sent him to St. Louis with utilityman Cookie Rojas and pitcher Jerry Johnson in exchange for catcher Tim McCarver, relief pitcher Joe Hoerner and center fielder Curt Flood. The latter refused to report, choosing instead to challenge baseball's reserve clause in a fight he lost. To replace him, the Cardinals later sent first baseman Willie Montanez to the Pacific Coast League farm club of the Phillies at Eugene, Oregon, in a transaction that ultimately was to help the Phillies considerably. Other moves saw the Phillies trade outfielder John Callison to the Chicago Cubs for relief pitcher Dick Selma and outfielder Oscar Gamble, and sign free agent pitcher Jim Bunning after his release by the Los Angeles Dodgers.

The new manager of the Phillies was 43-year-old Frank Lucchesi, who had managed in the minor league for 19 years, 14 in the Phillies system. Lucchesi lasted two and one-half seasons. His luck failed to match his enthusiasm and his popularity with the fans. Injuries plagued his teams, none of which came close to breaking even. In 1970 the Phillies again finished fifth despite a productive season by Deron Johnson, who was the regular first baseman in place of the departed Allen and who hit 27 homers and knocked in 93 runs. Effective relief pitching was turned in by right-hander Dick Selma and left-hander Joe Hoerner, who combined for 17 wins and 31 saves. Second baseman Denny Doyle and shortstop Larry Bowa came up from the minors to make the grade and Bowa stayed on to become a member of the 1980 world champions. The speedy Bowa, who became one of the most consistently effective fielding shortstops in baseball history, struggled at bat his first season, but Lucchesi stuck with the youngster when he was hitting below .200 and Bowa finished at .250.

Injuries, however, decimated the club again. Young Don Money, who had been moved from shortstop to third base to make room for Bowa, was leading the league with a .356 average on

May 21 when a bad-hop ground ball hit him in
the right eye and sidelined him for 27 games.
The worst day that season was on May 2 at San
Francisco when both of the club's catchers, Tim
McCarver and Mike Ryan, who had been the
first-string catcher the previous two years since
his trade by Boston, were seriously injured in the
same game and the same inning. First, a foul tip
off the bat of Willie Mays broke a bone in the
back of McCarver's right hand in the sixth
inning. Later in the frame, Willie McCovey slid
into Ryan at the plate and broke a bone in the
back of the catcher's left hand. Later that season,
even the two catchers brought up from the minors
to replace the regulars were hurt, forcing the
activation of Coach Doc Edwards for 35 games.
Ryan didn't return until mid-August, McCarver
not until September, and the Phillies, who were
in second place a month after the season opened,
faded and finished only half a game out of the
Eastern Division cellar. Before the next season
began, the Phillies enjoyed a change of scene,
moving into a new park.

The Phils close out their years in Connie Mack Stadium on this winning run in the 10th inning to beat Monteal, 2-1, on October 1, 1970. Tim McCarver is the player who scored the last run in the old stadium.

Steve Carlton was perhaps the premier player of the 1970's on what became a team of stars. He began his career as a Phillie in 1972 by capturing 27 of the team's 59 wins, including 15 in a row, and the Cy Young award. In 1980 he again won the Cy Young award, his third, along with 24 games, plus three games in post season play. In between he firmly established himself as the left handed pitcher of the era and the left handed strikeout king of all time. As the 1980's began, he seemed almost sure to become only the sixth pitcher to record 3000 strikeouts, and had an excellent shot at 300 career wins.

Chapter Nine

MIXED EMOTIONS

In the early 1960's the Phillies management began seeking alternatives to their home in outmoded Connie Mack Stadium with its deteriorating neighborhood and its lack of adequate parking. Owner Bob Carpenter at one point purchased land across the river in New Jersey with the idea of building a ball park. The city, having lost the Athletics, moved in and began planning for a stadium to house both the Phillies and the Eagles of the National Football League. Those plans came to fruition on Saturday afternoon, April 10, 1971, when the largest baseball crowd in the history of Pennsylvania turned out for the opening of the new Veterans Stadium. The 55,352 fans saw Jim Bunning pitch the Phillies to a 4-1 victory over Montreal. Although they drew a club record home attendance of 1,511,223 that year, the season went mostly downhill after the gala opener, and the Phillies finished sixth and last in the Eastern Division.

Willie Montanez, the first baseman obtained from St. Louis, was converted into a center fielder and enjoyed a banner rookie season with 99 runs batted in and 30 home runs, and first baseman Deron Johnson batted in 95 runs and hit a career high 34 homers. But the team as a whole was 11th in the league in runs scored, 12th in batting average and was ninth in team pitching. The pitching highlight was provided by Rick Wise, who won 17 games and pitched a no-hit game in winning, 4-0, on June 23 in Cincinnati. In that game, the right-hander became the first pitcher ever to hit two home runs in a no-hitter, and only a walk in the sixth inning kept him from pitching a perfect game.

In training camp the following spring, Wise was a holdout until the Phillies traded him for another holdout, St. Louis Cardinal left-hander Steve Carlton. That deal saved the strike-delayed 1972 season from being a complete disaster for the Phillies. Carlton led the league in almost every pitching category. He won 15 games in a row from June 7 through August 17 after losing six of his first 11 decisions. The longest such streak in club history finally ended when Phil Niekro and the Atlanta Braves edged him and the Phillies, 2-1, in 11 innings at the Vet on August 21 before 41,212 fans. He finished with a 27-10 record and a 1.98 earned run average, also leading the league with 30 complete games, 346 innings and 310 strikeouts. He was a unanimous choice for the Cy Young Award. Despite Carlton's brilliance, the Phillies, who were in a virtual tie for first place after 20 games, finished with the worst record in the league. Only one other pitcher won as many as seven games, and young left-hander Ken Reynolds tied a club record by losing 12 straight games before posting his first victory on September 1. Rookie left · fielder Greg Luzinski led the team with a .281 batting average, 68 runs batted in and 18 homers, and no other regular hit over .260.

Rick Wise is shown in a game of glory that comes to few pitchers. Here he is in the process of pitching a no-hitter against the Cincinnati Reds on June 23, 1971. He hit two home runs in the Phils 4-0 victory, the only pitcher ever to hit two home runs in a no-hitter.

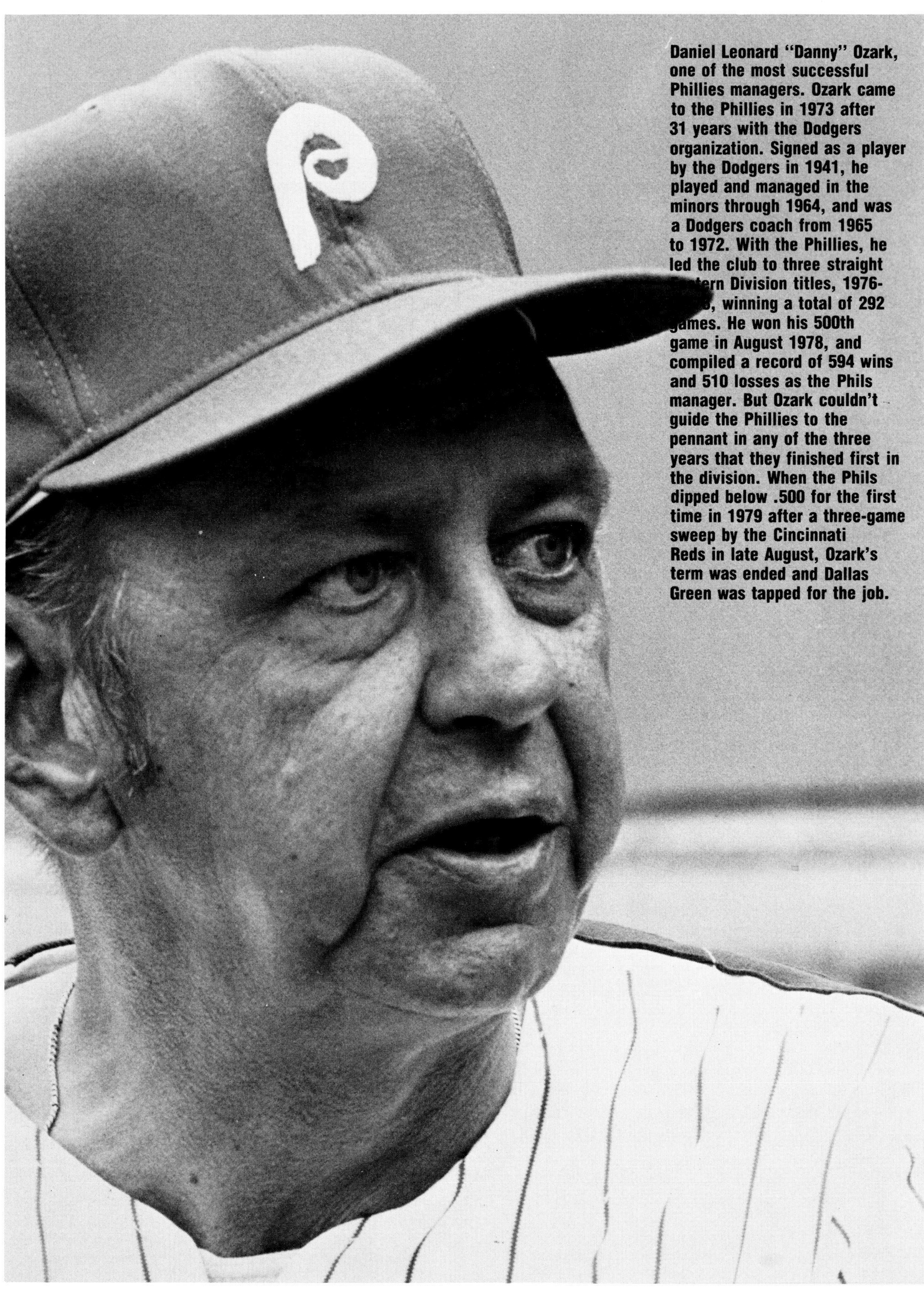

Daniel Leonard ''Danny'' Ozark, one of the most successful Phillies managers. Ozark came to the Phillies in 1973 after 31 years with the Dodgers organization. Signed as a player by the Dodgers in 1941, he played and managed in the minors through 1964, and was a Dodgers coach from 1965 to 1972. With the Phillies, he led the club to three straight Eastern Division titles, 1976-78, winning a total of 292 games. He won his 500th game in August 1978, and compiled a record of 594 wins and 510 losses as the Phils manager. But Ozark couldn't guide the Phillies to the pennant in any of the three years that they finished first in the division. When the Phils dipped below .500 for the first time in 1979 after a three-game sweep by the Cincinnati Reds in late August, Ozark's term was ended and Dallas Green was tapped for the job.

There were major changes in the club management in 1972. General manager John Quinn was replaced on June 3 by farm director Paul Owens, who had joined the organization in 1956 and worked as minor league manager and scout before heading the minor league organization. On July 10 Owens pulled a surprise by firing Frank Lucchesi and taking on the added duty of managing the team on the field. That didn't help the Phillies get out of the cellar, but Owens said it helped him evaluate his own players and those on the other teams in the league. "I learned a lot," Owens said. "I heard and saw things in the dugout I couldn't possibly have known if I hadn't been in uniform."

In late November, Bob Carpenter retired as president of the Phillies to become chairman of the board, and was succeeded by his son, Ruly, who at 32 was the youngest club president in the major leagues. Ruly, who had played football and baseball at Yale, had started working for the club in the fall of 1963 and had filled a variety of positions in preparation for his eventual takeover as president. Three weeks before that change, the two Carpenters and Owens had completed their search for a new manager, hiring long-time Los Angeles Dodger coach, minor league first baseman and manager Danny Ozark. The 6-foot, 2-inch Ozark, who turned 49 in the month he was appointed, had spent 31 years in the Dodger organization and was a great believer in the stressing of fundamentals. The affable Ozark weathered media and fan criticism in his early years and stayed around to guide the Phillies to three straight Eastern Division titles, the first of which occurred in 1976 when the team won 101 games and had a winning percentage of .626, both club records that were matched in 1977. Still, Ozark never won a pennant and, when the club skidded in 1979, he was fired.

In Ozark's first season of 1973, the Phillies finished sixth and last for the third straight year, although they added three players who were to play important roles in future successes. One was veteran pitcher Jim Lonborg, hero of the 1967 pennant-winning Boston Red Sox who was obtained in a trade with Milwaukee for third baseman Don Money. Two were rookies — third baseman Mike Schmidt and catcher Bob Boone. Had Steve Carlton pitched anywhere close to his 1972 form, the Phillies would have been in the thick of the Eastern Division race that saw five clubs finish within five games of each other, but the left-hander was a 20-game loser and one of four Phils who won 13 games.

Greg Luzinski continued to improve, pacing the offense with 29 home runs and 97 runs batted in. Utilityman Bill Robinson hit 25 homers and knocked in 68 runs. Schmidt had trouble making contact in his rookie year, batting only .196 and striking out more than one-third of the time, but he showed power with 18 homers and demonstrated an ability to play third base extremely well.

Immediately after the 1973 season, the Phillies obtained second baseman Dave Cash from Pittsburgh in a trade for pitcher Ken Brett, who had come from Milwaukee with Lonborg to win 13 games. Cash brought along a winning attitude, the ability to play second base and to hit in the leadoff spot. He coined the slogan, "Yes, We Can," that excited the fans enough so that a new attendance record of 1,808,648 was set. Despite

Del Unser has been one of the great pinch hitters, especially in the clutch games. Here he is driving a single to right field in a July 1973 game against the Chicago Cubs. The Phils went on to win that game, 7-4, and Unser at the time was leading the National League with a .345 batting average. He was with the Phils twice, once from 1973-74 and again from 1979-80. He recorded seven pinch-hit home runs, including a record three in a row in 1979.

inferior pitching and a June 5 knee injury that kept Luzinski out almost half the season, the Phillies were in first place for 51 days and as late as August 2, 1974, before fading to third. Willie Montanez, who had returned to full-time duty as a first baseman the year before, and Cash led the team in batting with averages of .304 and .300, and Schmidt blossomed as a slugger, leading the league with 36 home runs and finishing second in runs batted in with 116. Jim Lonborg won 17 games and Steve Carlton 16 to pace the pitchers.

Improving the bullpen was the top priority before the 1975 season and that was accomplished. In a December trade with the New York Mets, the Phillies acquired left-handed reliever Tug McGraw and, during spring training, a deal with Cleveland brought left-hander Tom Hilgendorf. These two combined with right-hander Gene Garber, purchased from Kansas City the previous July, to win 26 games and save 28. Steve Carlton won 15 games, rookie Tommy Underwood 14 and Larry Christenson 11. Lonborg, almost useless after mid-June because of an injury, won only eight.

On offense, the Phillies scored more runs than any team except pennant-winning Cincinnati. The team's .300 hitters included Dave Cash, part-time outfielder Jay Johnstone, left fielder Greg Luzinski and even shortstop Larry Bowa, the last three reaching that figure for the first time. Mike Schmidt led the league in homers again with 38 and batted in 95 runs, while Luzinski led the league in runs batted in with 120 and hit 34 homers. Two May trades brought in Garry Maddox to play center field and former Phil Dick Allen to play first base. Willie Montanez was

Veterans Stadium, whose baseball seating capacity was increased from just over 56,000 to more than 65,000 in its first 10 years, opened its gates for the first time to jubilant Philadelphia fans on April 10, 1971. The opening ceremonies are shown here. Before 55,352 fans that Saturday afternoon, the Phillies beat the Montreal Expos, 4-1.

A swing like this by Greg Luzinski often brought fireworks from the scoreboard, runs for the Phillies, and cheers from the fans for another "Bull Blast." The powerful Greg posted a career high .309 batting average, 39 home runs and 130 RBIs in 1977, has twice finished second in MVP voting and has appeared in four All-Star games. He started well in 1980 and was headed for another 30-plus home-run year before hitting a slump in June and injuring his knee in July. In the 1980 Championship Series, he hit the game-winning home run in the first game and the game-winning double as a pinch hitter in the fourth, and has hit safely in 15 of the 16 Championship Series games the Phillies have played.

dealt to San Francisco for Maddox, who was an immediate hit with his ground-covering strides and his speed on the bases. Two farm system prospects and cash went to Atlanta for Allen, who had refused to report to the Braves following his trade by the Chicago White Sox. Allen proved to be a disappointment in his two years with his old team.

The Phillies played championship baseball at home but were 11 games under .500 on the road. A seven-game winning streak in mid-May moved them into second place, but they promptly dropped six in a row on the road. They were second most of the season behind Pittsburgh, which lost 14 of its first 18 August games to give the Phillies hope. Although they won only eight of their first 17 games in August, the Phillies moved into a tie for the lead on August 18 with a 6-3 victory at Atlanta. The next night they fell one game back because of a ninth-inning loss to the Braves, triggering a slump that saw them lose 10 of their next 15 games. They went on to finish second, six and one-half games behind Pittsburgh.

When the Phillies reported for spring training in 1976, they were confident this would be the year they would finish on top. Their pitching staff had been bolstered by a pair of December

Dave Cash shows the form that led the majors with 213 hits in 1976 as the ball (far right) approaches. Cash came from the Pirates in October 1973 and immediately helped settle down a young Phillies infield. He led the National League in defense at second base in 1976 and helped the Phils move from last place in 1973 to third, second, and finally, first place in 1976.

Jim Lonborg was one of the Phillies top right-handed pitchers during the 1970s, especially 1974, 1976, and 1977. He holds the happy distinction of winning at Montreal on September 26, 1976, to give the Phils their first title since 1950.

trades that brought right-hander Ron Reed from
St. Louis and left-hander Jim Kaat from the
Chicago White Sox. In addition to these two
veterans, the bench was strengthened by the
signing of outfielder-first baseman Bobby Tolan
before the end of the exhibition season.

As they had the year before, the Phillies started
the 1976 season by losing three of their first four
games. A turning point came in the fifth game at
Wrigley Field on April 17 when the Phillies

Gene Garber doing what he did so well after coming to the
Phils in 1974: relieving. In this early season game in 1976,
he was called to the mound with men in scoring position.
Although the Phillies lost the Championship Series in 1976
to the Cincinnati Reds, Garber combined with Tug McGraw
and Ron Reed to win 24 games and save 36 while each
appeared in more than one-third of the team's games.

overcame 12-1 and 13-2 deficits to beat the
Chicago Cubs, 18-16, in 10 innings. Mike
Schmidt made history in this game by becoming
only the 10th player to hit four home runs in a
game and only the fourth to hit four in successive
times at bat. He homered in the fifth, seventh and
eighth innings, then hit a two-run homer in the
10th, finishing with eight runs batted in and five
hits in six at bats.

The Phillies took over first place with a 10-5
victory over Atlanta at home on April 24, but fell
to second the next day when they bowed to the
Braves, 3-2. After this defeat, Ozark lost his
temper for the first time in a post-game press
conference, ordered all members of the media out
of the clubhouse and even threatened to punch
one wire service reporter. Some of the players
felt that Ozark's eruption had cleared the air and
stirred the team. At any rate, the Phillies
completed that home stand by winning two out of
three games from Cincinnati, then swept a
three-game series at Atlanta and a two-game
home series with Houston. On May 9, they beat
the Los Angeles Dodgers for the second time in
three games at home and moved into the Eastern
Division lead to stay.

The Phillies posted a 22-5 record in May to
take a six and one-half game lead over
Pittsburgh, which stayed in the runner-up spot to
the finish. Ozark's club won 20 of 29 games in
June, 17 of 29 in July, and 14 of the first 24 in
August to assume their biggest lead, a 15½-game
bulge over the Pirates. Just when it appeared the
Phillies might set a record for the largest margin
ever for a division champion, they hit their first
sustained slump. The team which had lost as
many as four in a row only once previously
dropped eight straight games, starting on August
27 in Cincinnati. At the same time, Pittsburgh
was putting together a 10-game winning streak.
After the Phillies had lost their eighth in a row,
their lead was down to six and one-half games,
but Larry Christenson ended that skid on
September 5 at Shea Stadium by hitting two
home runs while pitching the Phillies to a 3-1
victory over the New York Mets.

The slump wasn't over, however. The Phillies
went to Pittsburgh and lost all three games
decisively, then came home to drop two of three
games to the Chicago Cubs for their 13th loss in
their last 15 games before Christenson again
came to the rescue. In the series finale with the
Cubs on Sunday, September 12, the right-hander
pitched a six-hit shutout to win, 8-0, and Steve
Carlton and Jim Lonborg made it three in a row

126

Tug McGraw uncorks a Cutty Sark. Most pitchers call their offerings fastballs, curves, or sliders. McGraw prefers names with a bit more panache. And fittingly so. Certainly he has the stats; he is the National League leader in career saves. But it is his style, his infectious enthusiasm, and his wit along with the stats that have made him a star. Incidentally, McGraw calls this pitch his Cutty Sark because it sails.

Jim Kaat begins his motion in a 1976 game. His years with the Phils, 1976-79, were only modestly successful, but he is recognized as one of the most underrated pitchers of the past 20 years, being among the all-time top 20 in victories (272), strikeouts, innings pitched, and games started, where he is No. 5. He also established a reputation as a great fielder, earning 16 consecutive Gold Gloves from 1962-1977.

A picture of awesome power gathered at the plate in 1976. Bobby Tolan is congratulated by the Phils bat boy as he crosses the plate after belting a home run. Mike Schmidt (20) congratulates Jay Johnstone who crossed the plate ahead of Tolan. Greg Luzinski (19) moves toward Tolan. Tolan, who played three outfield positions as well as first base, was signed as a free agent in March 1976.

with victories over Montreal, giving the Phillies a
six-game lead.

Pittsburgh came to the Vet then to sweep a
two-game series and the Phillies went to Chicago
and lost to the Cubs in the 12th inning on
September 17 for their 18th defeat in the last 23
games. That night the Pirates won at New York
for their 18th victory in the last 22 games, and
that sliced the margin between the two to three
games, the smallest it had been since May 22.

Steve Carlton beat Chicago the next day while
Pittsburgh was losing, and the Phillies won seven
of nine games to clinch the division title in the
first game of a September 25 doubleheader at
Montreal. Jim Lonborg pitched a four-hitter and
Greg Luzinski's three-run home run in the sixth
inning, his 21st of the season but only his first in
exactly one month, was the big blow in the 4-1
victory. The Phillies recovered well from their
long slump, won 13 of their final 16 games and

"Look out for The Bull." Greg Luzinski goes into second with determination and enough power to send the Pirates defender flying. The nickname "The Bull" seems particularly apt in this photo with Luzinski's arms almost looking like horns.

seemed to be ready for their first post-season series in 30 years.

That Championship Series with the Western Division champion Cincinnati Reds opened on October 9 at Veterans Stadium. The Phillies didn't win a game. Steve Carlton was knocked out of the box in the eighth inning of the 6-3 first game defeat; the Reds chased veteran right-hander Jim Lonborg in a four-run sixth inning and won, 6-2, in the second game after being held hitless for five innings while trailing, 2-0.

Veteran left-hander Jim Kaat started the third game following a day off and the shifting of the site to Cincinnati. The Phillies scored first for the third straight game as doubles by Mike Schmidt and Greg Luzinski produced a run in the fourth inning, and a walk and doubles by Garry Maddox and Schmidt made it 3-0 in the seventh. Kaat, who had allowed only one hit in the first six innings, was replaced by Ron Reed after an infield hit and a walk in the seventh, and the Reds scored four times in the inning to take a 4-3 lead, the last two runs scoring on a pop-fly triple by Cesar Geronimo. The Phillies bounced back to score two runs in the eighth and another in the ninth and Reed carried a 6-4 lead into the home ninth when lightning struck. After George Foster and Johnny Bench homered in succession to tie the score, Gene Garber relieved and, after Dave Concepcion singled, was replaced by left-hander Tommy Underwood, who issued two walks around a sacrifice to load the bases. Ken Griffey followed with a bouncer off the glove of first baseman Bobby Tolan to win the game and the pennant.

It was a bitter finish to the Phillies' best season since 1950, but there were plenty of highlights. Steve Carlton, reunited with his old St. Louis batterymate Tim McCarver, was a 20-game winner for the third time in his career; Jim Lonborg won 18, including his first eight

The sound of champagne corks popping was heard in the Phillies dressing room on September 26, 1976, when the team won the division championship under Danny Ozark, the first of three straight division titles.

decisions, and the bullpen trio of Gene Garber, Tug McGraw and Ron Reed combined to win 24 games and save 36 while each appeared in more than one-third of the club's games. Offensively, Mike Schmidt won his third straight home run title, hitting 38 and knocking in 107 runs. Garry Maddox hit .330, third high in the league, Jay Johnstone batted .318 and Greg Luzinski .304.

In some ways, the 1977 season was almost a repeat of the year before as the Phillies again won the Eastern Division title, won 101 games and lost the Championship Series. There were some changes on the roster, however. Second baseman Dave Cash had played out his option and signed with Montreal, and first baseman Dick Allen played out his option and signed with Oakland. To replace Cash, the Phillies traded reserve catcher Johnny Oates to the Los Angeles Dodgers for Ted Sizemore, and the Phillies signed Richie Hebner, a third baseman who had played out his option with Pittsburgh, and made

Greg Luzinski was one of the bright spots for the Phillies in the League Championship Series of 1976-78. Throughout the three years that the Phils were in the championship series, Luzinski recorded at least one hit in every game, posted at least one home run in each series, and was one of the team leaders in RBIs, being first in 1976 and 1977. The Reds catcher in this 1976 action is Johnny Bench.

Richie Hebner, dust-covered from a head-first slide, returns safely to base. Hebner was signed in December, 1976, by the Phils to play first base after playing out his option as a third baseman with the Pittsburgh Pirates.

him the first baseman. Veteran infielder Davey Johnson, who had played the previous two years in Japan, was signed to beef up the bench. Left-hander Randy Lerch and right-hander Warren Brusstar, who had been standouts on the Oklahoma City farm club in 1976, were added to the pitching staff, the latter as a reliever. One of the two trades they made on the night of the June 15 deal deadline also helped. In it, they obtained a leadoff batter and right fielder from St. Louis in Bake McBride.

Injuries to Richie Hebner, Jim Lonborg and Tug McGraw played a part in the Phillies' slow start in 1977. They lost six of their first seven games, took more than a month to reach the .500 mark, were still fourth in mid-June and were eight and one-half games behind the front-running Chicago Cubs as late as June 29. The Phillies started an eight-game winning streak on June 30, the first four at home against Pittsburgh. They then went to Pittsburgh and lost four straight. In the first game of that series on July 8, Mike Schmidt, who had hit 25 homers in the club's first 77 games, fractured the ring finger on his right hand in a fight involving Pirate pitcher Bruce Kison because of some knockdown pitches. Although he tried to play after that with a splint on the injured finger, the third baseman's swing was affected for the next six weeks. After the debacle in Pittsburgh, the Phillies came home to win two of three from St. Louis and three of four from Chicago to go into the All-Star Game break in second place, only two games back.

On August 5 the Phillies moved half a game in front by beating the Los Angeles Dodgers in the opener of a three-game home series for their third straight victory and remained in first place for the rest of the season. They swept the Dodger series, won three in a row from Montreal at home and went to Chicago and won all four games. A 7-4 triumph in Montreal on August 16 was the final victory in a 13-game winning streak that ranks as the longest in the club's modern history and was the longest in the National League in 11 years. The streak ended the next night when Steve Carlton was beaten, 13-0. The Phillies won 22 games and lost only seven in August, matching the club record for wins in one month, and won their 16th straight home game on September 3 against Cincinnati for another club record. The division-clinching victory came in Chicago on September 27 when Larry Christenson won his 18th game of the season and hit a grand-slam home run in a 15-9 triumph.

This time the Phillies were confident that the

Championship Series would bring them a
pennant. Again they came up short, this failure
being even more galling than the one in 1976.
All they managed to accomplish was to win their
first post-season game since Grover Alexander
beat Boston in the first game of the 1915 World
Series. The Phillies won the first game in Los
Angeles on October 4, scoring twice in the ninth
inning for a 7-5 victory. Greg Luzinski's two-run
home run in the first inning, first baseman Dave
Johnson's two-run single in the fifth that chased
Dodger ace Tommy John, and the run that pitcher
Steve Carlton singled home in the seventh gave
the Phillies a 5-1 lead. But Ron Cey hit a
grand-slam homer off Carlton to tie the score
before Gene Garber and Tug McGraw blanked
the Dodgers the rest of the way, and the Phillies
scored twice in the ninth off Elias Sosa on Mike
Schmidt's single and a balk to win. It was
Schmidt's lone hit of the series.

Ted Sizemore was obtained in a trade with the Los Angeles
Dodgers in December, 1976, after Dave Cash played out his
option and signed with Montreal. Sizemore ably filled
Cash's shoes at second. Here he's safe on an emphatic
call by the umpire and Phils coach Billy DeMars as Pete
Rose tries to make the tag. Rose was a nemesis of the
Phils while wearing a Cincinnati Reds uniform.

The Phillies were confident now because they knew they would go back home with at least a split in the first two games, and that's all they got when the Dodgers won the second game, 7-1. Don Sutton outpitched Jim Lonborg in this one and Dusty Baker hit a grand-slam homer in the fourth inning to snap a 1-1 tie.

The pivotal third game at Veterans Stadium was one the Phillies and the 63,719 fans will never forget. It ended in a sudden and bitter defeat. The Dodgers jumped off to a 2-0 lead in the second inning, but Dodger pitcher Burt Hooton lost his control in the home half of that inning. After giving up two singles, he walked four straight batters amid deafening cheers from the home fans. The last three bases on balls forced in runs to give the Phillies a 3-2 lead, but the Dodgers tied the score and chased starter Larry Christenson in the fourth on Ron Cey's double and Dusty Baker's single.

Warren Brusstar, Ron Reed and first-game

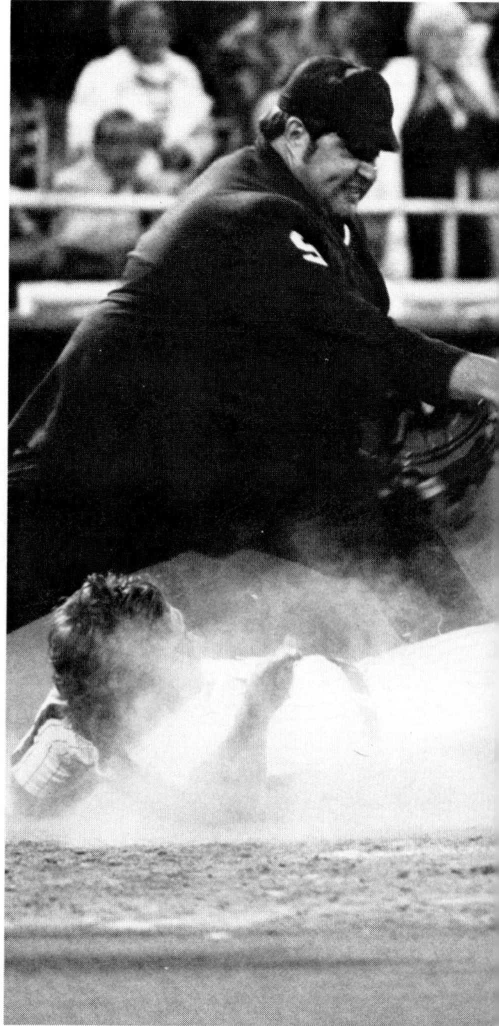

Tim McCarver hits the dirt in front of home plate to score in a Phillies 9-8 win over Houston on June 7, 1977. Frame I shows him heading for the plate as his leg starts to hook Houston catcher Ed Herrmann. Frame II shows McCarver safe, the catcher down, and the umpire pointing, indicating Tim has touched the plate. Frame III shows the official call "Safe" by the umpire.

winner Gene Garber held the Dodgers through the eighth when the Phillies broke through for a pair of runs on Richie Hebner's double, a run-scoring single to right by Garry Maddox and two Dodger wild throws. That gave the Phillies a 5-3 edge and the way Garber was pitching the lead seemed safe. The sidearming right-hander had retired the four batters he had faced in the first game and the first six batters who opposed him in this one, all without allowing a ball to leave the infield. When he set down Baker and Rick Monday on ground balls to start the final inning, the victory appeared secure.

Suddenly, however, the situation changed. Veteran Vic Davalillo batted for Steve Yeager and beat out a perfectly placed drag bunt to start the rally. Manny Mota batted for reliever Lance Rautzhan and Garber quickly got two strikes on him, but the veteran stroked an inside pitch to left field and Greg Luzinski started in, then went back. At the wall, the left fielder leaped and got his glove on the ball, but it caromed off the fence back into his hands for a double. When Luzinski's throw-in bounced away from second baseman Ted Sizemore, Davalillo scored and Mota took third.

Davey Lopes was next and third baseman Mike Schmidt moved in a step or two for the leadoff batter because "I was afraid with the tying run on third he might try to bunt his way on." Lopes didn't bunt, but hit a hard hopper that skipped off the heel of Schmidt's glove over to shortstop Larry Bowa, who grabbed the ball barehanded and threw to first. The play at first was extremely close, but Umpire Bruce Froemming ruled Lopes safe, a call the Phillies bitterly disputed. With the score now tied, Garber threw the ball past first trying to pick off Lopes. Bill Russell followed with a ground single up the middle to bring Lopes home from second with the run that won the game, 6-5.

Manager Danny Ozark was roundly

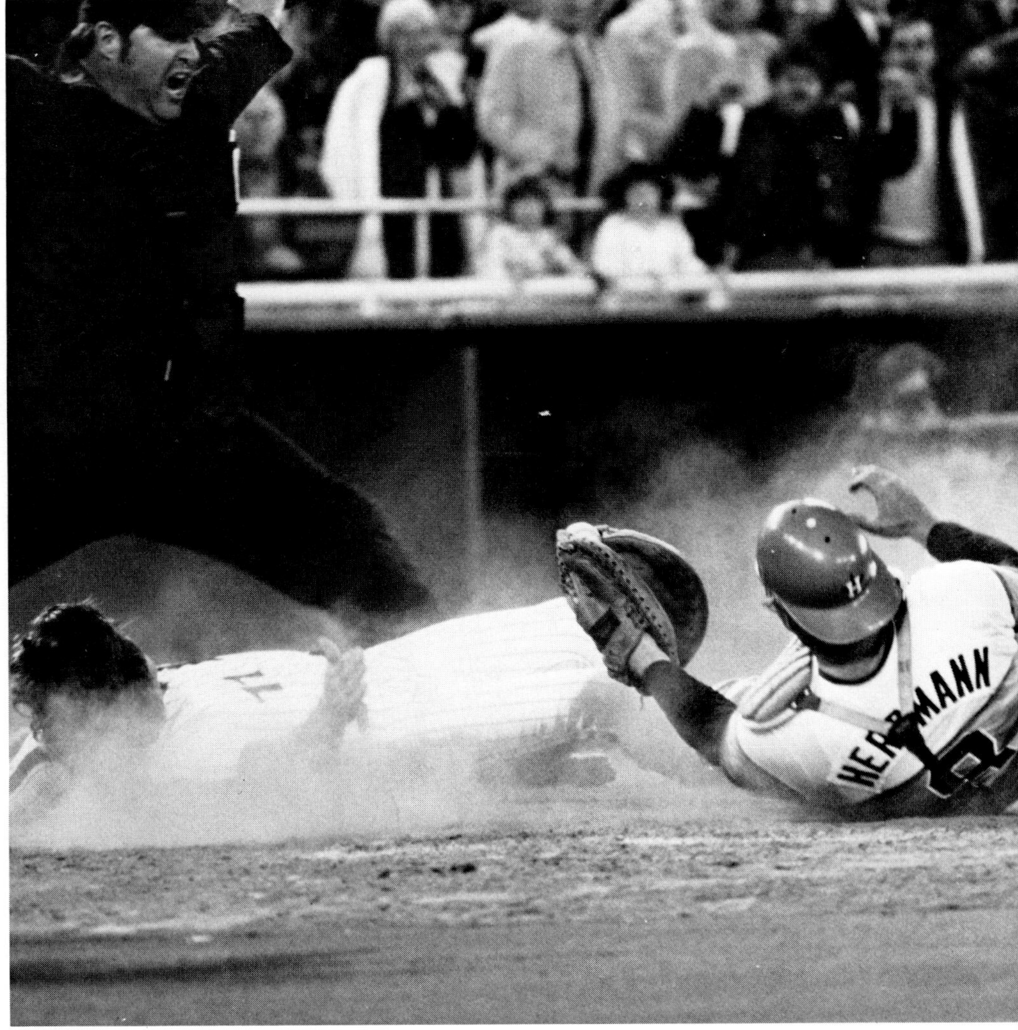

second-guessed by members of the media and by some of his own players for not inserting defensive specialist Jerry Martin in left field at the start of the ninth, a move he had made routinely all season long, and one that would have enabled the Phillies to win the game.

The loss of that game was a crushing blow, and the Phillies played like automatons the next night. In a game played in a steady rain, causing more controversy, and before 64,924 fans, the largest baseball crowd in Pennsylvania history, the Dodgers won easily, 4-1. Tommy John outpitched Steve Carlton and Dusty Baker again supplied the big blow with a two-run home run in the second inning.

Despite failing to win a Championship Series game for the second straight year, Steve Carlton had a big season, posting a 23-10 record and winning his second Cy Young Award. Larry Christenson won 19 games, Jim Lonborg 11,

Randy Lerch 10, and the bullpen quartet performed yeoman service to win 29 games and save 46. Greg Luzinski had his biggest year, hitting .309, finishing second in the league with 130 runs batted in and third with 39 home runs. Schmidt hit one less homer and batted in 101 runs, and the Phillies, seven of whom hit more than 10 home runs, led the league in batting average and runs scored.

The only major trade the Phillies made in 1978 sent reliever Gene Garber to Atlanta to bring back starter Dick Ruthven, and that June 15 deal helped the club win its third straight Eastern Division crown. It didn't bring the desired pennant, however.

In 1978, the Phillies moved into the lead for good on June 23 after sweeping a doubleheader from the Chicago Cubs at home. Although their lead was never bigger than five and one-half games, the Phillies appeared to be in no trouble,

Garry Maddox came to the Phillies in 1975 and established
himself as a peerless centerfielder. Through 1980 he has
won the Gold Glove six consecutive years with no sign of
letting up. Maddox is also a dangerous base runner, with
twenty or more stolen bases for eight consecutive years,
and a consistent threat at the plate compiling a .289 career
average. His best season was 1976 when he batted .330.
His biggest hit was the 5th-game, 10th-inning double to
drive in the winning run in the 1980 League Championship
Series against Houston.

especially after winning six of eight meetings with Pittsburgh in the first half of August to push the fourth-place Pirates 10½ games behind. The Bucs caught fire immediately after that, won 22 of their next 25 games and the Phillies went to Pittsburgh for the final four games of the season with only a three and one-half game lead. On Friday night, the Bucs won a doubleheader, and appeared headed for their 25th straight win at home on Saturday, September 30, when Willie Stargell hit a home run with the bases loaded in the first inning. However, with pitcher Randy Lerch hitting two home runs and Greg Luzinski hammering a three-run homer, the Phillies bounced back to win, 10-8, and wrapped up the division championship.

The Championship Series was another sad tale.

The Phillies again bowed to the Dodgers in four games, failing to win at home. Four home runs, two of them by Steve Garvey, helped the Dodgers win the opener, 9-5, on October 4. Left-hander Tommy John pitched a four-hit shutout to give the Western Division champs an easy 4-0 victory in the second game.

The next night in Los Angeles, Steve Carlton highlighted a four-run second inning with a three-run homer and later singled home what proved to be the winning run in the sixth in a 9-4 victory.

The end came the next afternoon when the Dodgers won, 4-3. The Phillies loaded the bases with none out in the first inning against left-hander Doug Rau and failed to score. A two-run homer by Greg Luzinski gave the Phillies

Bob Boone in a classic picture of his defense of home plate. The two-time Gold Glove winner (1978-79) was hampered by injuries in 1980, but found his old batting stroke in time to hit .412 in the World Series. In the division-clinching victory at Montreal, he singled with two out in the ninth inning to tie the game that Mike Schmidt won with a home run two innings later.

The stance of the power hitter. Mike Schmidt is set in the batter's box. Schmidt had his greatest season in 1980 when he was a unanimous choice for the National League's Most Valuable Player Award, and was also named MVP of the World Series. He homered in his last four regular season games in 1980, hitting the game-winner in the 11th inning at Montreal to give the Phillies the Eastern Division title, giving him a league-leading 48 for the season and an all-time record for homers by a third baseman. In addition to leading the league in homers for the fourth time in the last seven years, he also led the National League in runs batted in (121), in total bases (342), in slugging percentage (.624) and in total chances for a third baseman, winning his fifth consecutive Gold Glove.

a 2-1 lead in the third, but Ron Cey homered off Randy Lerch in the fourth to tie. Bake McBride's pinch homer in the seventh following a solo homer by Steve Garvey in the sixth left the score tied at 3-3 and the game went into extra innings.

In the home 10th, Tug McGraw who had retired the Dodgers in order in the ninth, walked Ron Cey with two out. Dusty Baker followed with a liner over second that center fielder Garry Maddox raced in to glove at his knees, but then dropped for an error. Two pitches later, Bill Russell singled to center and Cey scored with the run that won the game, 4-3, gave the Dodgers the pennant and the Phillies their third straight defeat in the Championship Series.

Despite the division title, the Phillies didn't do nearly as well individually in 1978 as they had in the previous two seasons. Steve Carlton led the pitching staff again, but won only 16 games as he had some soreness in his shoulder. Larry Christenson and Dick Ruthven each won 13 and Randy Lerch 11, while the bullpen duo of Ron Reed and Tug McGraw combined for 11 wins and 26 saves. The only regular to come close to hitting .300 was Larry Bowa, who had his best all-around season with a .294 average and his second Gold Glove Award as the best fielding shortstop in the league. Center fielder Garry Maddox hit .288, catcher Bob Boone and first baseman Richie Hebner .283. Powerwise, left fielder Greg Luzinski was the team leader, finishing fourth in the league with 101 runs batted in and second in homers with 35. Third baseman Mike Schmidt, hindered by leg injuries, fell off to 78 runs batted in and 21 homers and Hebner knocked in 71 runs and hit 17 homers. Things only got worse in 1979.

Dick Ruthven fires to a Cubs batter in a June 23, 1978, game, the first of a double-header. The Phillies swept both games and moved into first place for the rest of the season.

140

Jay Johnstone, Phils outfielder who was regarded as something of a "hot dog" on the diamond, is presented with a giant-size version of the same before a game with Houston. Charlie Franks holds the big-sized gift as Phillies executive vice president William Y. "Bill" Giles assists. Franks is a living legend at the Phils park where he has been dispensing hot dogs to fans for so long that he's been able to put two of his offspring through college on the returns from his hard work.

Davey Johnson receives a hero's welcome as he hits home plate in a key game against the Los Angeles Dodgers on June 3, 1978. Johnson came to the Phillies in 1977 as a free agent after playing for two years in Japan where he won awards for his hitting and fielding. In his season and one-half with the Phillies, he filled in at first, second and third base and contributed many clutch hits. In 1978, before being sold to the Chicago Cubs, Johnson became the first pinch hitter in major league history to hit two grand-slam homers in one season. Johnson starred for the Baltimore Orioles for more than seven years, then set a big league record for home runs by a second baseman when he hit 43 for the Atlanta Braves in 1973.

Mike Schmidt shows why he's a winner of five straight Gold Gloves and second to Brooks Robinson in *Baseball Magazine's* ''Third Basemen of the Decade'' Award. Always strong at the plate, here he handles a high, hard hop straight at him in a 1978 contest against Houston.

Steve Carlton warms up prior to one of his more than 500
starts. Unlike so many other left-handed strike-out artists,
Carlton has proven to be one of baseball's most durable
moundsmen.

Dallas Green, the man who took the Phillies to the World Series. Green pitched in 185 major league games with the Phillies, Washington Senators and New York Mets from 1960 through 1967, managed in the Phillies farm system for two years and then moved into the front office after the 1969 season as assistant to Paul Owens, Phillies director of minor league operations. He became farm director in 1972 when Owens moved up to general manager, then replaced Danny Ozark as the club's field manager on August 31, 1979. Although his managing style has been criticized by some of his players, he demanded all-out effort and that's what he got in 1980 — performance on a World Championship level.

Chapter Ten

WORLD CHAMPIONS AT LAST

The management of the Phillies was beginning to wonder if they would ever put together a team that would win a pennant after the third straight year in which the club won the Eastern Division title and lost the Championship Series. It seemed obvious that something was missing. The talent was obviously there, but something more was needed. When Pete Rose played out his option with the Cincinnati Reds and became a free agent, it was decided that he might supply the extra ingredient necessary for a pennant. The Phillies were one of the teams which selected the durable star in the re-entry draft, and they made what they thought was a substantial offer to him. There was deep disappointment when the Phillies found their offer was much less than other clubs were willing to give the future Hall of Famer.

Bill Giles, the club's energetic and capable executive vice-president was especially distressed by the apparent failure to land Rose, who was known to want to play for the Phillies for several reasons. Giles refused to give up, and began looking for ways to make the Phillies offer as attractive as some of the best ones Rose already had. Giles, brought into the organization after the 1969 season because of the many problems attendant on the club's imminent move into Veterans Stadium, figured out a way. He went to the television station which carried the games of the Phillies and got it to agree it would pay the ball club $600,000 more for the TV rights if Rose were a member of the team. With that additional revenue, the Phillies were able to offer Rose a four-year package worth approximately $3.2 million and, although some other clubs offered more, the hustling infielder accepted.

Rose, who had played regularly at second base, right field, left field and third base during his years with the Reds, was installed as the first baseman of the Phillies. Although he had never played there previously, he worked hard to learn his new job and before too long was acknowledged as a good first baseman. Overall, Rose had another excellent season; the Phillies did not. Part of the club's problem was an almost unprecedented string of injuries. The Phillies had been apparently strengthened by two other transactions in addition to the signing of Rose. In February they had traded second baseman Ted

Sizemore and two reserves, outfielder Jerry Martin and catcher Barry Foote, along with two young pitchers out of the farm system to the Chicago Cubs for second baseman Manny Trillo, a player they had once owned and long coveted, outfielder Greg Gross and catcher Dave Rader. In March, they sent Richie Hebner, whose first-base job had been taken over by Rose, to the New York Mets for right-handed pitcher Nino Espinosa.

When the season began, the Phillies appeared to be taking dead aim on their fourth straight division crown. After losing their first two games, both on the road, they began to win consistently, getting good hitting, pitching and defense. On May 17 the Phillies played another in their series of heavy-hitting games in Chicago, a trend begun in 1896 when Ed Delahanty hit four home runs in a game the Phillies lost, 10-9, and continued in 1922 in an all-time record 26-23 loss to the Cubs, and again in 1976 in the 18-16 victory that saw them overcome an 11-run deficit. The Phillies won this 1979 slugfest, 23-22, on a 10th-inning home run by Mike Schmidt after the Phillies had frittered away a 17-6 advantage.

This victory gave the Phillies a record of 24-10 for the season and a four-game lead in the division. But just when all seemed rosy, the bottom dropped out. The Phillies came home and promptly lost three straight games to Montreal and failed to win as many as three games in a row until July 4. By July 1, they had fallen to fifth place, seven and one-half games in back of first place, and their record was only one game over .500. By winning 12 of 16 games between July 2 and July 20, the Phillies climbed to within two games of the lead, but a pair of six-game losing streaks in the next two and one-half weeks doomed their chances. When the club's record dipped below the .500 mark for the first time August 28 during a three-game series sweep by Cincinnati at Veterans Stadium, it was decided a managerial change had to be made. On August 31, shortly after the club reached Atlanta, it was announced that Dallas Green was moving from his post as the club's farm director to the dugout as manager, ending Danny Ozark's term of almost seven years during which the club won 594 games, tied one and lost 510, and won three

Pete Rose does it all. Rose batting left. Rose batting right. Rose with his patented hallmark — a head-first slide. No matter which side of the plate he hits from, the result is the same: a bear-down, all-out player who is a constant threat. Once on base, he's a hell-for-leather player, running, stealing, sliding. Always competing. His stats would fill a book: records for hits, home runs and total bases by a switch-hitter; the modern National League record for hitting in consecutive games (44); the only player ever to get 200 or more hits in a season 10 times. He has played regularly at second base, right field, left field, third base and finally first base, where he led the league in fielding percentage in 1980 with only five errors in 1,555 total chances. He made the next to last putout in the final World Series game with his patented hustle, catching Frank White's foul pop when it bounced off the glove of teammate Bob Boone.

division titles. Green, who had pitched for the Phillies, Washington Senators, New York Mets and San Diego Padres in the major leagues, and managed in the Phillies farm system before moving into the front office after the 1969 season, guided the club to 19 victories in its last 30 games, but the team won only 84 games and finished fourth, 14 games behind Pittsburgh. Despite their poor showing, the Phillies broke their home attendance record, drawing 2,775,011, a figure only the Los Angeles Dodgers have ever surpassed.

The injury list was a long one that season. Pete Rose was the only regular who wasn't sidelined by some physical problem. Manny Trillo missed 46 games with a broken arm after being hit by a pitch; Greg Luzinski missed 26 with leg injuries; Bob Boone 23 with a broken finger and then a bad knee that required surgery late in the season, and Larry Bowa 16 with a thumb injury. Of the pitchers, Larry Christenson, Warren Brusstar, Randy Lerch, Tug McGraw and Dick Ruthven all were afflicted. On July 4, Ruthven and Christenson were placed on the disabled list and the night before Lerch suffered a broken right wrist in a mugging.

Pete Rose played in all 163 Phillies games that year, batted .331 by hitting .421 in September, collected more than 200 hits for a record 10th time, stole a career-high 20 bases and hit safely in 23 straight games, the best such streak in the major leagues that season. Mike Schmidt set a club record with 45 home runs to finish second in the league and batted in 114 runs. Greg Luzinski fell off to only 18 homers and 81 runs batted in while hitting a subpar .252. Larry Bowa hit only .214 but set an all-time record for highest fielding percentage of .991 by a shortstop, making just six errors. However, he failed to win a Gold Glove, although teammates Schmidt, Bob Boone, Manny Trillo and Garry Maddox did. Among the pitchers, Steve Carlton won 18 games, Nino Espinosa 14 and Randy Lerch 10 to pace the starters, while Ron Reed, with 13 victories and

five saves, and Tug McGraw, with four wins and 16 saves, topped the relievers. The inability of Warren Brusstar to pitch in more than 14 innings because of shoulder soreness hampered the bullpen staff.

Although Green had originally taken the managing job on an interim basis, he decided he'd like to try it for a full season, a decision that pleased both owner Ruly Carpenter and general manger Paul Owens. All three made it clear, however, that Green had no intention of becoming a career manager, that he intended to return to front-office work as soon as practicable and to follow the plan that would have him eventually succeed Owens in the general manager's spot.

The trio also agreed that the poor showing in 1979 was not sufficient reason to begin making wholesale changes. The nucleus of the club remained the same, but Green did insist on promoting some of the top prospects in the minor league system, cutting loose some of the veterans to make room on the roster. The rookies included players like catcher Keith Moreland, infielder Luis Aguayo, outfielders Lonnie Smith and George Vukovich and pitchers Dickie Noles and Scott Munninghoff. Moreland, Smith and Noles played significant roles in the subsequent winning of the world championship, as did pitchers Bob Walk and Marty Bystrom, who joined the club during the season.

The strike of the players in the contract dispute with the owners that cancelled the final week of the exhibition season may have contributed to a slow start by the Phillies, who compiled only a 6-9 record in April and were for the most part

Like a vacuum cleaner, Larry Bowa's glove sucks in another ground ball. Bowa holds the major league record for the highest fielding percentage for a shortstop in a lifetime (.981) and in a season (.991). He also holds the World Series record for starting double plays: seven.

The Phillies Garry Maddox and the Pirates Willie Stargell, standing side by side, symbolize their two teams. Like the players, the Phils and the Pirates have been close to the top of the National League Eastern Division since 1974: the Phillies have finished in first place four times and the Pirates have been close to the top three times. From 1975-1978, these two Pennsylvania rivals finished in the top two spots in the division.

playing inconsistent baseball. Things began to pick up in May as they won 17 and lost only nine, held first place briefly on two occasions and finished the month only one game back. June was marked by a six-game winning streak, ended up as a break-even month, although the Phillies went into July only two games in back of division-leading Montreal.

During July, Steve Carlton broke the major league record for strikeouts by a left-handed pitcher in a career and Mike Schmidt became the most prolific home run hitter in the club's history when he hit the 260th of his career. Also during July the Phillies actually moved into first place very briefly, but they went into August in third place. On August 8, they opened a four-game series in Pittsburgh, and lost every game, including a Sunday doubleheader August 10 and

Keith Moreland is one of the Phillies bright young stars of the future. Although he can play first base, third base and the outfield, the Phillies have employed him primarily as a reserve catcher and here he stretches to make a tag at home plate against the Los Angeles Dodgers. In 1980, he hit .314 in the regular season, then batted .333 as the designated hitter in three World Series games. He hit his first major league home run off Cincinnati's Tom Seaver in May and his first big league grand-slam homer off Bill Gullickson at Montreal in June. His all-out hustle and grind-it-out style were hallmarks of the Dallas Green-managed Phillies down the stretch in 1980.

that dropped them six games back. Between games of that twin bill, Green really laid out the troops with a verbal attack that players described later as classic.

Whether Green, who had not minced words all season long about the shortcomings of some of his players — to the discontent of several of them — stirred the team with his speech or not, the fact is that the Phillies began to play better. They went into Chicago and beat the Cubs twice in three games, and went to New York and won all five games with the Mets. Although they won only two more games than they lost in August, they went into September trailing by just half a game, then won 19 and lost 10 in September and the first four in October to clinch the division crown.

On Monday night, September 29, the Phillies won a game that may well have been the turning point for the stretch drive. In the opener of a four-game series with the Chicago Cubs, the Phillies overcame a 5-3 deficit with three runs in the bottom of the 15th inning to win, 6-5. They won the next three games from the Cubs and headed for Montreal and the final weekend of the regular season knowing they had to win two of the three games to beat out the Expos for the division title. Just the weekend before, Montreal had come to Veterans Stadium and won two out of three games to knock the Phillies out of the lead.

The Phillies went into the climactic series confidently. Their starting pitching rotation was set, and relievers Tug McGraw and Sparky Lyle, obtained September 13 from the Texas Rangers, were pitching effectively. In addition, third

Manny Trillo (9), Larry Bowa (10), and Pete Rose (14) execute the run-down perfectly with Rose tagging out the Pirates Omar Moreno.

Steve Carlton is shown here opening the Phillies 1980 season against Montreal. The Phils won the opener, 6-3, and returned to finish the regular season against the Expos. Carlton, along the way in 1980, won his third Cy Young Award with a 24-9 season plus three post-season wins and he became the all-time left-handed strikeout pitcher on July 6, 1980, when he fanned Tony Scott for his 2,933 strikeout.

baseman Mike Schmidt was hitting the long ball consistently.

The Phillies won the series opener, 2-1, on October 3 as Dick Ruthven posted his 17th victory with help from Lyle in the seventh and McGraw in the eighth, and the hitting of Schmidt. The third baseman hit a sacrifice fly to give the Phillies a 1-0 lead in the first inning, then his 47th homer of the season in the sixth.

The Saturday afternoon game was delayed more than three hours by rain. When it was played, it was almost as sloppy as the weather. There were seven errors in the game and 18 men left on base. The Phillies were one out away from defeat when catcher Bob Boone singled home the tying run in the ninth inning. With McGraw again blanking the Expos, the Phillies won in the 11th, 6-4, when Pete Rose singled

Steve Carlton tips his hat to a standing ovation from the fans as the message board says it all on August 22, 1980.

and one out later Schmidt delivered again, hitting his 48th homer into the left seats. That blow also broke the major league record for home runs hit in one season by a third baseman.

Schmidt not only led the major leagues with his 48 homers, he also led the National League in runs batted in with 121 and his .286 batting average was the highest of his big league career. He was the unanimous choice as the league's Most Valuable Player, the third member of the Phillies to win that award. Right fielder Bake McBride had the most productive season of his career, batting in 87 runs while hitting .309. Pete Rose's average dipped to .282 but he led the league with 42 doubles, and Manny Trillo had his best season, batting .292. Rookie outfielder Lonnie Smith played in 100 games, batted .339 and stole 33 bases to break Richie Ashburn's club

Larry Bowa steals second against the Astros in this action from 1980. He has stolen 20 or more bases for seven consecutive years. Obviously a dangerous runner, Bowa has had three inside-the-park home runs.

record for a rookie, while Keith Moreland hit .314 in 62 games.

Left-hander Steve Carlton had his best season in eight years, postings a 24-9 record, a 2.34 earned run average and leading the league in strikeouts and innings pitched as well as in victories. He won his third Cy Young Award for his efforts. Dick Ruthven had his best season with 17 victories, and Tug McGraw was the top reliever with five victories and 20 saves and was at his best the last half of the season. Two rookies, Bob Walk who was called up from the minors in late May, and Marty Bystrom, who was promoted on September 1 from Oklahoma City, also contributed substantially. Walk won 11 games despite some control problems and Bystrom won all five of his decisions while giving up just six runs in the 36 innings he worked.

The Phillies had to wait until after Monday's playoff game in Los Angeles to find out their opponent in the Championship Series, and before the first game against the Houston Astros on Tuesday night, October 7, at Veterans Stadium they learned that their requests to replace two of their pitchers had been granted. Marty Bystrom went on the roster in place of Nino Espinosa, who was able to pitch in only 12 games during the season because of bursitis in his shoulder, and left-handed Kevin Saucier replaced Randy Lerch.

Steve Carlton pitched the opening game of the Championship Series. Despite not being at his best, he beat the Astros, 3-1, with relief help from Tug McGraw over the final two innings. He also was aided by the two-run home run that Greg Luzinski hit in the sixth inning to overcome Houston's 1-0 lead. Greg Gross, batting for Carlton in the seventh inning, singled home the game's final run off loser Bob Forsch.

In the second game, Dick Ruthven opposed Houston's Nolan Ryan before the second straight record crowd, this time 65,476 jamming Veterans Stadium. A walk, a sacrifice and Terry Puhl's single to left gave Houston a 1-0 lead in the third inning. The Phillies moved ahead, 2-1, in the fourth when Mike Schmidt and Greg Luzinski doubled, Manny Trillo sacrificed and Garry Maddox singled to left. Unusually wild, Ruthven walked his fifth batter in the seventh and the Astros tied the score. With two out, Ryan was allowed to bat despite the score, and Ruthven walked him. Puhl then doubled to bring the pitcher home.

McGraw, who came on after Ruthven left for a pinch-hitter in the seventh, gave up a run in the eighth on Joe Morgan's double and a single by

Sparky Lyle, former great Yankees reliever, was acquired late in the 1980 season to take some of the pressure off Tug McGraw. In Lyle's first appearance for the Phillies here against the St. Louis Cardinals on September 14, one day after he was picked up from the Texas Rangers, he gave up four runs, two earned. He didn't give up another run until his final appearance on October 4.

Jose Cruz, but the Phillies tied in their half on two singles around a sacrifice, Garry Maddox knocking in the run. The Phillies, who had left the bases loaded in the seventh, stranded Maddox and Larry Bowa, who was issued an intentional walk, in the eighth when Bob Boone struck out against reliever Dave Smith and pinch-hitter Del Unser flied out. With Frank LaCorte pitching for Houston in the ninth, the Phillies muffed a chance to win the game after Bake McBride and Mike Schmidt singled. Lonnie Smith looped a single to right and McBride, who appeared certain to score, was instead stopped at third by Coach Lee Elia. Then with the bases loaded, LaCorte struck out Manny Trillo and retired Garry Maddox on a pop foul.

Against Ron Reed, who had pitched the ninth for the Phillies, the Astros scored four runs, then stopped a budding rally by the Phillies to win, 7-4, and square the series. A single by Puhl started the Houston uprising and a two-run triple by Dave Bergman ended the scoring. In the home 10th, after the Phillies scored once, aided by a wild throw, Joaquin Andujar retired Mike Schmidt on a fly ball on a 3-0 pitch with two runners on base to end the game.

John Vukovich symbolizes the Phillies 1980 effort through the regular season, the league championship series, and the World Series. The team had to scratch and claw its way to the top, relying on the kind of extra effort shown here by Vukovich as he successfully dives for third base in advance of an oncoming Mets runner. Infielder Ramon Aviles is in the background.

After a day off, the series resumed Friday in Houston's Astrodome with Larry Christenson and Joe Niekro opposing each other. Christenson retired for a pinch-hitter in the seventh after pitching six scoreless innings. Niekro pitched 10 scoreless frames before being lifted for a pinch-hitter. Both teams had scoring chances during regulation time, but it wasn't until the

home 11th that Houston scored to win the game, 1-0. Tug McGraw, who had come on to replace Dickie Noles when the Astros threatened in the eighth, gave up a leadoff triple to Joe Morgan in the 11th. After two intentional walks, Denny Walling lifted a sacrifice fly to left that scored pinch-runner Rafael Landestoy with the run that gave Houston a 2-1 lead in the series.

The Phillies had their backs to the wall when Carlton opposed Vern Ruhle in the fourth game on Saturday. A 20-minute argument in the top of the fourth inning over whether Ruhle had trapped or caught a soft looper off the bat of Garry Maddox cooled off Carlton, who gave up single runs in the fourth and fifth innings. Enos Cabell doubled to open the home fourth and eventually scored on Art Howe's sacrifice fly. Luis Pujols tripled off the center field wall and scored on Landestoy's single in the fifth to give Houston a 2-0 lead.

Six outs away from losing their fourth Championship Series in as many tries, the Phillies suddenly rallied, scoring three times in the eighth inning in a rally started by a single by pinch-hitter Greg Gross. Third-game winner Dave Smith relieved Ruhle and gave up singles to Lonnie Smith, Pete Rose and Mike Schmidt, tying the score. After Joe Sambito relieved, Manny Trillo lined a sacrifice fly to right that scored Rose with the run that made it 3-2. Trillo's ball was actually trapped by right fielder Jeff Leonard but right field umpire Bruce Froemming ruled it a catch, setting off another argument.

In the ninth inning, the Astros tied the score against the fifth pitcher for the Phillies, Warren Brusstar, who started the inning by walking Landestoy. A sacrifice and Puhl's single to right brought in the run that sent the game into extra innings for the third straight time. Rose started the winning rally for the Phillies in the 10th when he grounded a single to center with one out. One out later, pinch-hitter Greg Luzinski lined a double to left and Rose scored, although the ball beat him to the plate. The relay from Landestoy, however, was in the dirt and Rose scored before catcher Bruce Bochte could pick up the ball. Manny Trillo then doubled home an insurance run and McGraw retired the Astros in order in the home 10th to preserve the 5-3 victory that squared the series.

In the final game on Sunday night, the Phillies had to come from behind again. Rookie Marty Bystrom started against Nolan Ryan, and gave up a run in the first inning on a single by Puhl, who

Marty Bystrom was recalled from Oklahoma City on September 1 and was named the league's Pitcher of the Month with five starts and five wins. The Phils also won the Championship Series game and the World Series game in which he started, even though he had no decision in either.

This was the scene time and time again in 1980: Pete Rose in scoring position and Mike Schmidt at the plate preparing to register another RBI.

stole second and eventually scored with two out on a double by Jose Cruz. The Phillies took a 2-1 lead in the second when Bob Boone singled to center with two out to score Manny Trillo, who had singled, and Garry Maddox, who had walked.

A two-base error by Luzinski on a liner to left by Walling and a single to center by pinch-hitter Alan Ashby tied the score in the Houston sixth after two Astros had been thrown out at the plate trying to score in the second and fifth innings. In the seventh, Christenson relieved and was charged with three runs. Singles by Puhl and Walling around an intentional walk scored one run with two out and Art Howe tripled to right center as the first batter to oppose Reed, giving Houston a 5-2 advantage.

Again the Phillies were just six outs away from defeat when they rallied, scoring five times in the eighth inning. Larry Bowa singled to center, Boone singled off Ryan's glove and Gross laid down a perfect bunt toward third to load the bases. Rose walked to force in one run, and another scored when pinch-hitter Keith Moreland bounced to second into a forceout after Ryan had been replaced by Joe Sambito. Forsch then relieved and struck out Schmidt but Del Unser batted for Reed and singled to right to tie the score and Trillo tripled into the left field corner to give the Phillies a 7-5 lead. Against McGraw in the home eighth, singles by Craig Reynolds, Puhl, Landestoy and Cruz tied the score again.

Against Frank LaCorte in the 10th, the Phillies scored the run that gave them the 8-7 victory on a bad-hop double to right by Unser and a double to center by Maddox. Dick Ruthven, who had had relieved for the first time all season and retired the Astros in order in the ninth, did it again in the 10th and the Phillies had won their first pennant in 30 years. Trillo, who batted .381 and had starred both offensively and defensively, was named the Most Valuable Player of the Championship Series before the Phillies flew home the next morning to get ready for the World Series against the American League champion Kansas City Royals.

During the pennant celebration, owner Ruly Carpenter said, ''What's especially nice is that I've never seen a game where so many people contributed. And the fact that Garry Maddox got the game-winner is the most satisfying of all. I know in the back of his mind and the fans' mind was the ball he dropped in the playoffs two years ago in Los Angeles.''

The Phillies got home early Monday afternoon,

held a brief workout and met the American
League champion Kansas City Royals in the
opening game of the 77th World Series Tuesday
night, October 14, before 65,791 fans at Veterans
Stadium. Because the series with the Astros went
the full five games while the Royals were beating
the New York Yankees in three straight games in
the AL Championship Series, the Phillies were in
a bind for pitching. As a result, rookie
right-hander Bob Walk pitched the World Series
opener against Dennis Leonard, the 20-game
winner for the Royals, and posted the Phillies
first World Series victory since 1915, ending a
losing streak of eight games.

   A two-run homer by Amos Otis in the second
inning and a similar blow by Willie Aikens in the
third gave the Royals a 4-0 lead, but the Phillies

**A gigantic American flag is unfurled as part of the opening
ceremonies for the 1980 League Championship Series
matching the Phillies and the Houston Astros. Dramatic as
the ceremonies may have been, they were no match for the
series itself which saw four of the five games go into extra
innings.**

Greg Luzinski rounds the bases after belting a home run against Houston in Game No. 1 of the Championship Series. His bat helped the Phils win the pennant. In addition to this home run that won the first game, Luzinski pinch hit a double to drive Pete Rose home for the winning run in Game No. 4.

Two former Cincinnati Reds meet in championship play. The Phils Pete Rose dives into second base as his former Big Red Machine teammate Joe Morgan, playing for the Astros, dives after him. Rose was caught stealing on this play in the third inning of Game No. 5.

erupted for five runs in the home third in a rally started by Larry Bowa, who singled with one out, stole second and scored on Bob Boone's double to left. Lonnie Smith's single, a hit batsman, a walk and Bake McBride's three-run home run over the right field fence gave the Phillies a 5-4 lead. They chased Leonard with another run in the fourth on Manny Trillo's single, an error and Boone's second double. A walk and a hit batsman around McBride's single and a sacrifice fly by Garry Maddox made it 7-4 in the fifth, and the Royals were stymied by McGraw, who replaced Walk after George Brett doubled and Aikens hit his second home run of the game in the eighth to make the final score 7-6.

The Phillies came from behind for the fourth straight game to win the second game of the World Series on Wednesday night when Steve Carlton pitched for the home team against left-hander Larry Gura. The game was scoreless until the home fifth when designated hitter Keith Moreland beat out an infield hit with one out to start a two-run rally. Maddox doubled down the left field line, Trillo's sacrifice fly to right scored one run, and the second scored when Bowa singled to left.

The Royals had runners on base in each of the first five innings but didn't score until the sixth, aided then by an error. A single by Otis and a walk to John Wathan was followed by a high hopper Aikens hit to second. Trillo threw the ball past first, allowing Otis to come home, cutting the Royals deficit to a run, and they then scored three times in the seventh for a 4-2 lead.

Carlton, unusually wild, walked Willie Wilson to start the eighth and one out later loaded the bases by passing both Dave Chalk and Hal McRae. Otis brought in two runs with a double down the left field line, and Wathan hit a sacrifice fly to score McRae.

Gura was removed after six innings, and Royals relief ace Dan Quisenberry retired the Phillies easily in the seventh, but lost the game in the eighth. A walk to Boone, pinch-hitter Del Unser's run-scoring double, an infield out and McBride's single to right tied the score. Mike Schmidt doubled to right for another run and came home when Moreland singled to center, and Ron Reed retired the Royals in the ninth to protect the 6-4 victory for Carlton and the Phillies.

After an off-day, the Series switched to Kansas City, and in the third game on Friday night the Royals won the first World Series game in their history. Dick Ruthven opposed Royals

right-hander Rich Gale. The Royals got off in front when George Brett hit a solo home run in the first inning. Brett had left the second game in the sixth inning because of a problem with hemorrhoids, but had minor surgery performed the next day. The Phillies tied the score, 1-1, in the second on singles by Trillo and Bowa, a walk to Boone and Lonnie Smith's infield out that Gale fumbled momentarily.

The Royals moved ahead again in the fourth when Aikens tripled to left and came home on McRae's single to center. Again the Phillies came back to tie, this time when Schmidt homered to

Pete Rose lets no one stand in his way of a big score in Game No. 4 of the Championship Series. Here he drives right through Astros catcher Bruce Bochy to score on a pinch-hit double by teammate Greg Luzinski for the go-ahead run in the 10th inning to force the teams into Game No. 5.

left field to start the fifth inning. Otis homered for the Royals in the seventh, and the Phillies tied the score against reliever Renie Martin in the eighth. An infield hit by Bowa, who stole second and scored on a two-out single to right by Pete Rose, produced the Phillies run. Quisenberry relieved Martin then and blanked the Phillies through the 10th, but McGraw, who replaced Ruthven at the start of the home 10th, lost the game in that inning. U.L. Washington singled and Willie Wilson walked to start the rally, but the former was thrown out trying to steal as Frank White missed a bunt attempt. Wilson held first on the play but then stole second, setting up an intentional walk to Brett. Aikens ended the game with a single to left center and the Royals had won, 4-3.

On Saturday afternoon, the Royals made quick

Manny Trillo swings on his way to MVP of the league Championship Series. He batted .381 for the series and had perhaps his most outstanding game in Game No. 5. Defensively he cut down a potential run at the plate and his two-run triple put the Phils ahead, 7-5.

It was a long time between hugs and champagne. Phillies manager Dallas Green hugs coach Ruben Amaro and puts his arm around celebrating Pete Rose after the Phils won the pennant for the first time since 1950 — 30 long years.

work of Phillies starter Larry Christenson, chasing him in the first inning, scoring four times and setting up a 5-3 victory behind the pitching of Leonard and Quisenberry. Wilson started the rally in the first with a single to center and took third on a wild pickoff throw by Christenson. Brett tripled to right one out later and trotted home when Aikens hit his third homer of the Series. McRae and Otis doubled to make it 4-0 and Dickie Noles replaced Christenson, giving up Aikens' fourth homer of the Series in the second inning. The only real excitement after that occurred in the fourth inning when Noles threw a high, inside two-strike pitch to Brett that forced the third baseman to hit the dirt in a hurry. The knockdown also brought Royals Manager Jim Frey out of the dugout to protest. Both teams were warned and that ended the knockdown pitches for the Series.

The Phillies scored single runs in the second, seventh and eighth innings and Quisenberry relieved Leonard in the eighth and earned a save with two scoreless innings. Singles by Maddox and Bowa around an infield out and a throwing error gave the Phillies an unearned run in the second. Maddox scored in the seventh, hitting a double to right, moving up on Bowa's single and scoring on Boone's sacrifice fly that Wilson caught against the left center field wall. In the eighth, Rose doubled to left center, finishing Leonard. An infield out and Schmidt's sacrifice fly to right scored him. Unser then singled to right but Maddox grounded out and Quisenberry retired the Phillies on three ground balls in the

Two of the giants of the game stand side by side during the 1980 World Series. Pete Rose holds Kansas City's George Brett close to first in World Series play.

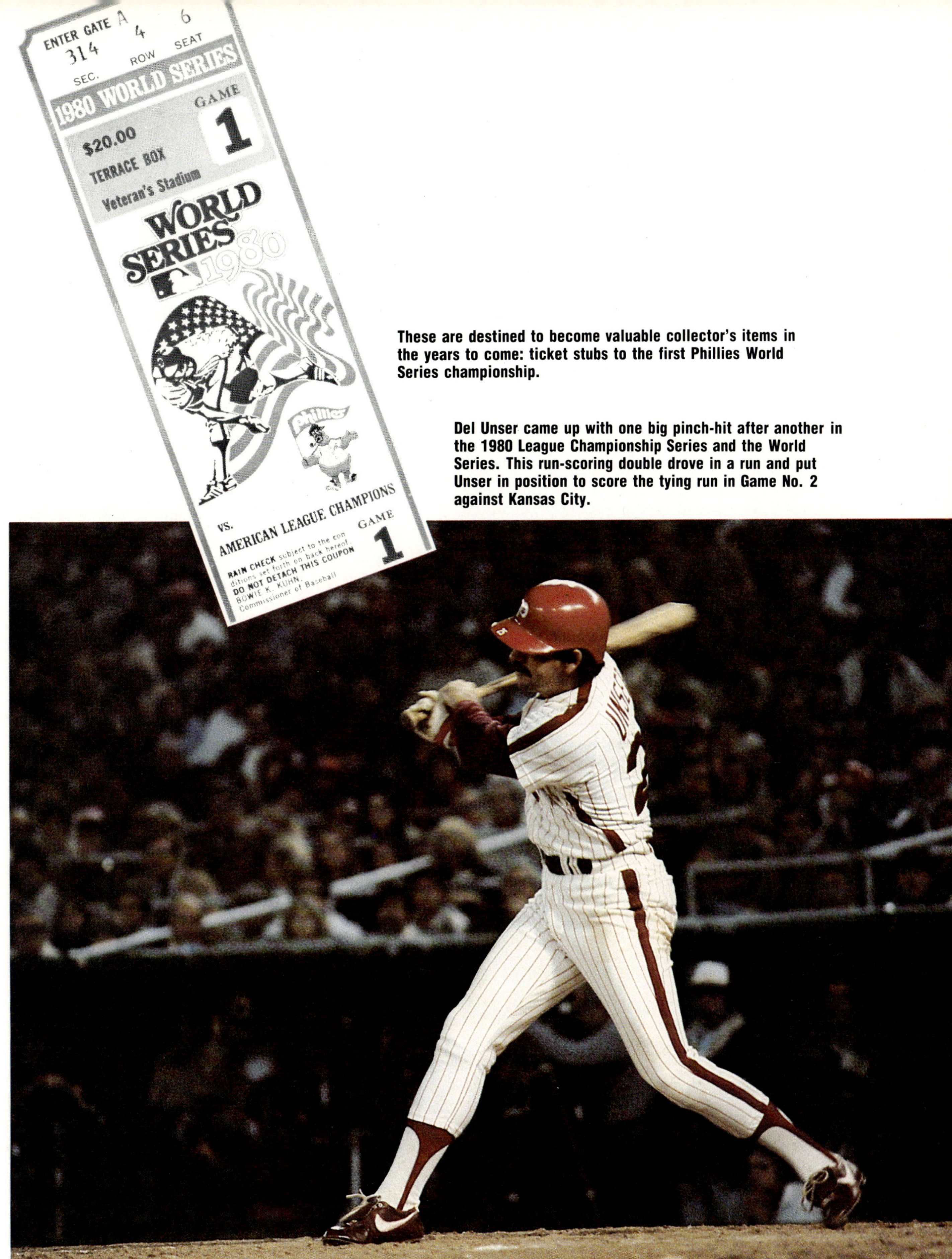

These are destined to become valuable collector's items in the years to come: ticket stubs to the first Phillies World Series championship.

Del Unser came up with one big pinch-hit after another in the 1980 League Championship Series and the World Series. This run-scoring double drove in a run and put Unser in position to score the tying run in Game No. 2 against Kansas City.

ninth.

With the Series tied at two games apiece, the fifth game on Sunday was vital. Green was forced to use another rookie as his starting pitcher, nominating Marty Bystrom to oppose Larry Gura. An error and Schmidt's home run over the fence in right center gave the youngster a 2-0 lead. The Royals got one run back in the fifth on singles by Washington and Wilson, a sacrifice and Brett's infield out. They scored twice in the sixth, chasing Bystrom, and going in front, 3-2. A home run by Otis to left center, and singles by Clint Hurdle and Darrell Porter brought Ron Reed to the relief of Bystrom. A sacrifice fly to left by Washington brought Hurdle across with the run that put the home team ahead. A great relay throw by Trillo after Wilson doubled nailed Porter at the plate for the second out of that inning.

Quisenberry had replaced Gura in the seventh and went into the ninth with a 3-2 lead when the Phillies rallied for the winning runs. Schmidt led off with a single off Brett's glove at third, and scored when Unser batted for Lonnie Smith and doubled to right. A sacrifice, an infield out, and Trillo's single off the pitcher's glove put the

With this swing, Mike Schmidt drove in the winning run in the second game of the World Series. This was one of seven RBIs to go along with two homers, a .381 average and, as a result, MVP honors in the Series.

Close plays at home plate were one of the big differences in the winner and the loser of the 1980 World Series. In Game No. 5, the Phils cut down John Wathan at the plate trying to score on a double by Willie Wilson. Bake McBride's throw in from the outfield was relayed by Manny Trillo to Bob Boone for the out — a key play in the one-run win. Here, however, the Phils show how to successfully run the bases. Bake McBride beats the throw to Wathan to score Game No. 2's winning run on Mike Schmidt's eighth-inning double.

Phillies ahead, and Tug McGraw kept them there. He survived a tense ninth in which he issued three walks but struck out Jose Cardenal to end the game and earn the 4-3 victory.

With two men on base and one out in that inning, McRae gave the left-handed relief ace a momentary jolt when he hit a ball down the left field line that curved foul. ''I probably would have had a heart attack,'' said McGraw later, when asked about the drive that almost ended the game.

That victory sent the Phillies back home with the confidence that they were finally going to win it all. They had Carlton and Ruthven ready to pitch and they had the advantage of the vocal backing of their home fans who had waited so long for a championship. Carlton was opposed by Gale in the sixth and final game on Tuesday night, October 21, at Veterans Stadium before 65,838 fans, another all-time record for a baseball game in Pennsylvania.

In contrast to the second game when he obviously was not sharp, Carlton was at his best in this game for the first seven innings, giving up just three hits, all singles, and two walks until the eighth, and allowing only one Royal to reach second in that time. The Phillies, on the other hand, chased Gale in the third inning, scoring twice. A walk to Boone opened that inning and he was ruled safe on a routine force play at second because shortstop Washington was past the bag. Rose laid down a perfect bunt for a hit that loaded the bases and Schmidt brought in the two runs with a single to right. That helped the third baseman, who had batted only .208 in the Championship Series, win the Most Valuable Player Award for the World Series.

Ron Reed (42) raises his arm in triumph as he saves Game No. 2 of the World Series for the Phillies. Reed saved the game to preserve the win for Steve Carlton and the Phillies by a score of 6-4.

Martin replaced Gale then and was tagged for a run in the fifth. Lonnie Smith led off with a ground double to center, took third on Rose's fly to center and, after Martin walked Schmidt and was replaced by Paul Splittorff, scored when McBride hit a slow roller to shortstop for the second out. A two-out double to left by Bowa and Boone's single to center gave the Phillies a 4-0 lead in the sixth.

The way Carlton was pitching, that appeared safe enough. But the Royals wouldn't quit. When Wathan walked to open the Kansas City eighth and Cardenal followed with a single to left, McGraw was again summoned from the bullpen, marking his ninth appearance in his club's 11 post-season games. The left-hander retired White on a foul pop to first, walked Wilson and gave up a sacrifice fly to center by Washington that

Larry Bowa pokes an opposite-field double to left with two out in the sixth inning of Game No. 6.

Larry Bowa goes high in the air after scoring the Phillies fourth run in the sixth inning of Game No. 6 in the 1980 World Series.

Mike Schmidt runs toward a jubilant Tug McGraw to share that championship feeling. The Phillies needed a lineup full of heroes to win, but certainly these two were at the head of the list for their clutch play down the stretch and in the World Series.

brought Wathan home with the only Royal run. Brett followed with an infield hit, but McRae grounded out with the bases loaded to end the inning. The bases became loaded again in the ninth on a walk to Aikens with one out, and consecutive singles by Wathan and Cardenal. White then lifted a foul pop beyond the Phillies dugout past first base and Boone got his glove on the ball. The catcher couldn't hold it, but the alert Rose grabbed it before it hit the ground. Now there were two outs.

With the huge crowd on its feet, cheering every pitch, police horses and police dogs ringing the field to prevent the fans from coming on the field after the final out, McGraw made four pitches to Wilson and struck him out to end the game. The 4-1 victory had given the Phillies their first world championship in their 98-year history,

and the old town erupted.

"This is the proudest I'll probably ever be as a baseball player," the jubilant McGraw said in the madhouse that was the Phillies clubhouse. Manager Dallas Green, who had bruised a lot of egos in goading his players to perform to the limit of their capabilities, said, "I'm proud of all these guys . . . . This team showed more guts the last month of the season than any team ever."

The celebration of that first championship continued throughout the night, and the next day more than a million Philadelphians turned out to watch their newest heroes parade down Broad Street to John F. Kennedy Stadium. There, some 85,000 gathered to hear brief speeches by the players and other members of the organization. It was a moment to be savored by all the Phillies personnel and all their fans, as well.

Somewhere in that crowd is Frank Edwin "Tug" McGraw who had just struck out Willie Wilson for the final out of the final game of the World Series 1980, bringing the World Championship Trophy to the City of Brotherly Love.

Tug McGraw holds up the headline that everybody knew: The Philadelphia Phillies had beaten the Kansas City Royals for the World Championship of Baseball. Philadelphians lined the 90-minute parade route that took the team from Market Street to Broad Street, past Veterans Stadium, and finally into Kennedy Stadium. There, McGraw and his teammates thanked the fans for their support and shared their sense of pride. Said McGraw at one point, "I'll bet that W.C. Fields is rolling over in his grave wishing that he was here with us. And I betcha 'ole Ben Franklin is somewhere having a couple of Irish whiskies and saying, 'I'm with you.' "

PHILLIE PHANATICS

The Philadelphia Phillies fan is perhaps the most famous in baseball. He knows how to cheer; he knows how to boo. And since the Vet opened, he knows that's the best place to do both. Philadelphia ranked second in attendance in the major leagues each season from 1976-80 averaging better than 2.5 million fans a year. Championship baseball along with hot dogs, hat day, Kiteman and the Phanatic all add up to one indisputable claim — Phillies baseball is phun!

Marlboro
971
408

P

PUBLISHER'S NOTES

The publisher wishes to express sincere thanks to the entire Philadelphia Phillies administrative staff for their wholehearted cooperation in allowing access to the Phillies photographic and team files. The wealth of material that we found in those files contributes significantly to this volume.

While we are unable to single out every individual on the Phillies staff, special thanks to Public Relations Director Larry Shenk, who gave us advice and guidance in tracking down some of the unique photographs in this book.

Without Executive Vice President William Y. Giles' approval and encouragement, we would not have undertaken this project. We are grateful to him.

Paul Roedig, Phillies team photographer, deserves a special mention for his assistance.

We are also indebted to Bill Loughman of Elmhurst, Illinois, who owns an extensive collection of baseball photographs, and Paul Hill of Philadelphia, who has a large collection of baseball pictures and memorabilia. Both enthusiastically contributed time and effort as well as materials.

JCP Corp. of Virginia
Publisher

Author's Acknowledgements

I would like to extend my thanks to a friend and a former great ball player, Richie Ashburn, who generously agreed to write the introduction to this work.

My personal thanks and appreciation also go to Executive Vice President William Y. Giles and Public Relations Director Larry Shenk for their encouragement and their cooperation in helping me to put down on paper the rich history of their team, the Philadelphia Phillies.

I also want to thank Joseph Dunn for his direction, help and editorial assistance.

To my wife Betty, I give thanks for her patience and understanding.

Allen Lewis
Author